Scrivener Superpowers

Scrivener Superpowers

How to Use Cutting-Edge Software to Energize Your Creative Writing Practice

M.G. Herron

Copyright © 2016 by M.G. Herron. All rights reserved.

This publication may not be reproduced without express written consent. The author appreciates your time and attention. Please consider leaving a review or telling your friends about this book, to help spread the word.

Scrivener Superpowers: How to Use Cutting-Edge Software to Energize Your Creative Writing Practice
www.ScrivenerSuperpowers.com

Thanks for your support.

ISBN: 978-1546445975
Second Edition

Written by M.G. Herron

www.mgherron.com

Published with The Write Practice
www.thewritepractice.com

Cover design by Jonathan Kurten
www.jonathankurten.com

For The Write Practice Community—
who made this book possible.

Table of Contents

Part 1: Introduction

Scrivener Superpowers	13
The Main Benefits of Scrivener	17

Part 2: Interviews with Authors

Conversations about Scrivener	23
Joanna Penn	24
Garrett Robinson	26
Gwen Hernandez	29
Joe Bunting	32
Rachel Aaron	34
Simon Whistler	36

Part 3: For Mac: How to Write a Story in Scrivener

A Walkthrough of Scrivener's User Interface	41
How to Structure Your Story	52
How to Create Character Sketches	60
How to Create Setting Sketches	67
How to Storyboard Your Story	74
How to Start and Finish a Draft	84
How to Set Targets and Measure Your Progress	90
How to Use Metadata and Stay Organized	100
How to Revise Your Story	107

113	How to Compile Your Story
137	Scrivener Tips for Pros

Part 4: For Windows: How to Write a Story in Scrivener

147	A Walkthrough of Scrivener's User Interface
158	How to Structure Your Story
165	How to Create Character Sketches
172	How to Create Setting Sketches
178	How to Storyboard Your Story
188	How to Start and Finish a Draft
195	How to Set Targets and Measure Your Progress
204	How to Use Metadata and Stay Organized
212	How to Revise Your Story
218	How to Compile Your Story
240	Scrivener Tips for Pros

Part 5: Additional Resources

251	Amplify Your Word Count
253	My No Nonsense Novel Template
254	Lester Dent's Pulp Paper Master Fiction Plot Template
255	How to Make Your Own Scrivener Templates
256	Further Reading Recommendations
259	About the Author
265	Notes and References

PART 1
Introduction

Scrivener Superpowers

Rock Bottom

A couple years ago I bottomed out. Despite my best efforts, I reached a low point in my writing practice the likes of which I had never seen. I had writer's block. I couldn't finish anything.

I had finished stories before, of course, but my story ideas always came in a burst of inspiration that seemed to fall out of the sky and onto the page through the force of some divine power. Those inspired moments make many writers fall in love with storytelling in the first place. I'm no different.

If you've ever experienced it yourself, you know how unreliable that kind of lightning strike is. The real challenge is trying to write something when you aren't inspired, when you have nothing to start with and don't know where you're going. That's the stuff that makes artists and true professionals. Not the lightning strikes, but the hard work and stick-to-itiveness required for a daily creative practice of any kind.

I despaired and stayed up nights thinking about how to overcome my block. I wrote in notebooks, in minimalist word processors, in Microsoft Word, and in Google Docs. I scrabbled desperately to climb up from rock bottom by sheer force of will.

I started a dozen more stories. I hated them all. I never finished a single one.

I returned to my study of story craft and listened to every writing and publishing podcast I could get my hands on. I scoured the collective knowledge of writers everywhere for a way forward. If I could just finish a draft, I thought, I would be able to make my way from there.

In this time of deep soul searching I discovered that the

biggest names in indie publishing were using a program called Scrivener to write their books. Not the piddling short stories I was trying to finish, but novels! Entire series! The projects I had only dreamed of attempting. They weren't just using Scrivener, either. They were *raving* about how amazing it was.

I'm not the type of person who buys into hype easily. Yet the topic of Scrivener kept cropping up. You know how it is when you hear about something new for the first time and it strikes a chord in you? In the following days and weeks, you suddenly see it everywhere you look. Social scientists call this "the frequency illusion," and I got it hard with Scrivener.

I was desperate, so I decided to give it a try.

What I discovered changed my life.

What Is Scrivener?

In simple terms, Scrivener is writing software. If you've ever used Microsoft Word or Google Docs or any other word processing software, you'll be familiar with many of its features. At a basic level, you type words in it and customize the appearance of those words on the page.

To get a little more technical, Scrivener is designed for drafting and structuring long-form content with a focus on helping you get to the end of your first draft.[1]

Isn't that funny? A piece of software that was designed to help writers do exactly what I found myself incapable of doing when I discovered it.

Scrivener is a word processor, an organizational and productivity tool, and an ebook compiler all in one. To think about Scrivener as "just another writing oftware" would be a mistake. To see why, you have to understand the paradigm that most modern writing software follows, and how Scrivener breaks the mold.

The Next Evolutionary Stage of Writing Software

Like all technology, writing tools have evolved by leaps and bounds over the last several hundred years. We went from scrolls to notebooks to typewriters to digital screens in a remarkably short amount of time, evolutionarily speaking.

Until Scrivener came along, however, the same *linear* paradigm was used: A single column of text was broken into pages to make length manageable. As technology advanced from manual to mechanical to digital, newly invented writing tools were based on the same linear paradigm we've been using since humans first wrote on vellum scrolls. When Macintosh was designing their operating system, for instance, they actually used a diagram of a scroll to explain the infinite canvas[2] of a digital screen. It made sense to base new technology on familiar paradigms. People adopt new software faster and with less resistance if the programs behave as expected.

I suspect that's why so many writers who have attended the workshops I've done on how to use Scrivener say that they just don't "get" it, that it's "not for them," or that the interface is "confusing." They say that because Scrivener doesn't behave in the same way as the word processors they are used to. I've helped many of these people get over that learning curve, and with this book I can help you do the same.

What makes Scrivener special, and the reason those big names in indie publishing rave about it and rely on it in their daily practice, is that it breaks the mold of the linear paradigm we've been using for so long.

As a result, using Scrivener effectively requires a new way of thinking. Despite the learning curve, it gives writers a great advantage. It allows you to work in a *nonlinear* way. You can manipulate the structure of a document to maximum effect, keep all your work in the same place, and much more.

The Lightbulb Moment

I, too, experienced a moment of confusion when I first saw Scrivener's interface. Fortunately, I have always been comfortable with technology and I love learning new software. My confusion quickly melted away and what I experienced next was nothing short of an epiphany.

Using the tools that Scrivener provides, which I'll go over in detail in Part 3: How to Write a Story in Scrivener for Mac and Part 4: How to Write a Story in Scrivener for Windows, I immediately began to finish my drafts. My writer's block evaporated because I had a tool to help me break my story down and figure out what was missing. Beyond that it was simply a matter of stringing sentences together until I reached every writer's two favorite words: THE END.

Don't get me wrong, those first drafts were terrible and many have never seen the light of day. I quickly realized that I needed to join writing groups, ask others for feedback, and eventually hire editors to take my work to the next level. Scrivener isn't a magic bullet that's going to make you an amazing writer overnight. It will, however, give you the power to take your story across the finish line, which is the first step to success.

I've published three short stories and a novel since my landmark discovery. This book was also conceived, written, and compiled with Scrivener.

And I'm not the only one. In Part 2, I interview several successful authors about how Scrivener fits into their writing process and makes a difference in their lives.

The Main Benefits of Scrivener

Now you know about the finishing power of Scrivener and how it helped me at a crucial time in my writing journey. So what else is the program capable of? Why should you try it if you can already finish a draft without it?

I believe that every writer, no matter how sophisticated or experienced, can find something in Scrivener to help him or her in a daily practice. For those that have never used it, the main benefits of Scrivener can be summarized in four high-level points:

1. **Versatility.** Scrivener provides an organized writing space that can be customized to suit your needs in each phase of the writing process.
2. **Structure.** Multiple view modes allow a manuscript of any size to be handled with ease. Instead of a cumbersome cut and paste process, restructuring is as easy as drag and drop.
3. **Organization.** Integrated metadata and productivity tools such as labels, statuses, and word count targets make keeping organized simpler than ever.
4. **Compilation.** The Compile feature generates publishable ebooks and print book files directly from a finished manuscript with a minimal amount of effort.

The gain in efficiency made possible by Scrivener is a huge boon to writers today, who live in a world where ebooks and self-publishing have revolutionized the publishing industry. This book will teach you how to get the most out of this cutting-edge software. In a few instances, I also include my own methods to fill in the gaps.

Get Organized

I'll show you how to apply story craft methods in Scrivener such as storyboarding, character sketches, setting sketches, and a process for revising your work.

I'll teach you to apply metadata to your story such as point of view and draft status. I'll guide you in the proper use of Snapshots to version control your drafts, and demonstrate how to use backups to remove the fear of losing your work.

Also, you'll learn why scenes are the basic unit of storytelling and how to structure your Scrivener file in a focused way according to this principle.

Amplify Your Productivity

When they're used correctly, word count targets in Scrivener are great positive encouragement. Rely on the carrot, not the stick, to stay motivated. Small achievable goals, notifications, and progress bars will keep you energized in a way that staring down a wall of words never could. I'll also teach you a method for tracking your progress over time that allows you to identify when you're most productive.

Spot problems early by manipulating your manuscript's structure. The earlier you can see and resolve issues with your story, the less time you'll spend rewriting and editing your work.

Lastly, spend less time and money formatting books. With Scrivener, there's no need to maintain separate files or pay a formatter to do what you can do with Compile in a few clicks.

SCRIVENER SUPERPOWERS

Take Your Writing Across the Finish Line

My method for finishing a draft is straightforward: sit down every day and put words on the page until you reach the end. I recognize, however, that every writer's process is different. Some people write out of order. Maybe you like to write the opening scene, then the climax scene, then the ending before going back to fill in the rest. With Scrivener, I'll show you how to work according to your *own* process.

Once your manuscript is done, I'll walk you through Compile so you can generate files for editors, beta readers, or publication. Plus, I'll show you a few advanced tips that will make your lives a whole lot easier.

The additional resources in Part 5 will also help you take your writing to the next level. Use my No Nonsense Novel Template to kickstart new stories, and explore the further reading recommendations for extra opportunities to learn.

PART 2
Interviews with Authors

Conversations about Scrivener

In the interviews that follow, I speak to six authors who use Scrivener for their work. We talk about why they switched to Scrivener from alternative writing software and how they use the program in their daily writing practice.

Each of these authors is at a different level of experience, success, and technical savvy, which provides a good cross-section of viewpoints. I hope the passion they exude sparks your creativity and gives you plenty of ideas for ways to refine your own process.

Each chapter includes a summary of the interview with key takeaways plus a link to watch the complete interview video on YouTube.

Joanna Penn

Bestselling author, professional speaker, and creative entrepreneur Joanna Penn credits Scrivener with helping her to mature as a writer. "It really is one of those life-changing tools for people and I think it's brilliant. I'm a real evangelist for Scrivener!" Joanna says.

On the road to becoming a full-time writer, Joanna has learned a lot and shares her knowledge with fellow authors in her nonfiction books and on her website, The Creative Penn.

The discovery of Scrivener came in 2012 for Joanna, just after she had finished her first fiction book. Prior to that all her writing was done in Microsoft Word. Her method of writing out of order was "a nightmare" in Word, so Scrivener's drag and drop feature won her over immediately. "As soon as I learned that you could throw stuff in and drag and drop the files around, that was it. All was solved."

As with many authors who write for a living, Joanna often has many projects on the go, and Scrivener helps her to organize her ideas and her workload. "I'm working in and around seven or eight projects at the same time," she says.

Although Joanna uses only about 20% of the features that Scrivener has to offer, she has found a system that works for her. "Basically, with a novel I will usually dump one liners of probably ten scenes. I don't heavily outline at the moment. Once I know the first 20,000 words I will then start the first draft. I will either be in a library or café and I'll open Scrivener." From here she uses the word count feature and writes around 2,000 words or a complete scene at each sitting. Once this process is completed and she has a first draft, she marks each scene with a yellow flag to show it is ready for editing.

"When all the flags are yellow, I print out the whole book, and do my first edit by hand, and then I will enter all the changes back into Scrivener," she says. Once happy with the edit, she changes each flag to blue, then compiles it to Word and sends it to her editor, who marks it up using Track Changes. "Then I will manually enter those into Scrivener, because one, I want to learn, but two, I don't want to necessarily use all the edits. I do those edits, then change the flags to green, then I will have a proofreader do the same process. And then I publish."

The compile feature allows Joanna to self-publish her books in different formats without the need to hire a formatter. This is one of the main reasons she recommends Scrivener to fellow authors. "If you're self-publishing, you should have Scrivener. It's just a no-brainer," she says.

For Joanna, Scrivener has become an indispensable tool. She has found a method that works for her and has become more organized as a result. "I'm quite happy with my process and I think I'm pretty productive," she says. You can learn more about how Joanna uses Scrivener, including access to a forty-minute behind-the-scenes video, when you sign up to her email list. Plus, you can get tons of other writing and self-publishing tips on her website at www.thecreativepenn.com.

Watch the full interview on YouTube.[3]

Garrett Robinson

Garrett Robinson is a prolific independent author who published over twenty-five titles in 2013 alone. Coming from a

background in the film industry, he is a self-taught expert on self-publishing and shares his knowledge with others through online video tutorials, blogs and podcasts. His work on the *Nightblade* dark fantasy series was also recently acquired by Sterling and Stone, a small independent press.

While working as a freelance filmmaker, Garrett wrote a number of scripts that he hoped to take to the big screen and direct. It's a tough industry to break into, though, and when a friend and fellow writer, Zach Bolger, suggested he turn his scripts into books, Garrett agreed. "So then I began writing. And he turned me onto *The Self-Publishing Podcast* and that's where I first heard about Scrivener. And I got it and just started learning everything I could about the program—because it's incredibly powerful."

Garrett has used Scrivener to write all his books, and uses it alongside Celtx when writing film scripts. "When I do a film project now I will generally have my Celtx project in which the script writing happens, but I actually do still use a Scrivener file because I use my research folder with links to websites and everything like that. Because that's a functionality that Celtx doesn't have. In fact I've never really seen a word processor, except for Scrivener, that does that."

When writing his novels, Garrett has a fine-tuned method. "How it starts is a very, very simple concept for the book. Just what's called the logline—in one or two sentences, what is the book? And then it's just taking the simple, core concept that is at the center of the book and expanding it and expanding it and expanding it, until I have an outline that is detailed. And then I take all of those beats, I put them in the binder and I start actually writing the first draft of the book." Using his "story beats" he creates a detailed outline and is able to write his first draft very quickly.

During the draft writing process Garrett relies on Scrivener's word count feature to help him track and improve his productivity. He has discovered he is at his most productive when working in hour-long chunks. "I'll generally write between 2500 and 3500 words an hour. And I keep track of my hours. I have my word counter sitting there and I always have it set for a goal for this hour of 2500 words." He also snaps a picture of the Scrivener screen word counter and posts it to his social media as way of keeping his fans posted on his progress

For the developmental editing stage, Garrett uses Scrivener's Compile feature to export the files to an ebook. He reads through the entire manuscript on his Kindle, making notes, then he goes back to Scrivener and makes structural changes. Next, he works on the copyediting, directly in Scrivener to get his phrasing right, before reading through the book in Scrivener again to check for typos and other errors. Finally, he records all his books to audio and includes this as the last stage of editing. "Reading a book out loud is the best way in the world to catch errors," he says.

He has learned the ins and outs of Scrivener so that he can continually improve his productivity and get the most out of all the program has to offer. This is especially true when it comes to the formatting and publishing stage, and Garrett has discovered many shortcuts and ways to improve how the final product looks. He uses metadata tags for his formatting rather than compiling "as is," which saves time and can produce a better final result. Metadata is something he strongly encourages all writers who are using Scrivener to better understand. "It's hard to tell people a specific usage for it, because it's so powerful and versatile and everybody's book will be different. So I feel like the best advice is to Google how to use Scrivener metadata and just start fussing around with it. Play around with different options for your book and you'll really swiftly discover, *Oh my god! This thing will change the way I format my books.*"

For the YouTube series *Authorpreneur Nuts & Bolts* Garrett collaborates with Sterling and Stone, and they work in a shared Scrivener file to write the scripts. Once the writing is done, Garret uses the Compile feature to export the script to a Kindle file. "That goes on my iPad and that's what I use as my little teleprompter when I'm filming the show. That's just one other way to use it. It's a damn versatile program."

Garrett's books, films, blogs and vlogs can be found on his website at www.garrettbrobinson.com.

Watch the full interview on YouTube.[4]

SCRIVENER SUPERPOWERS

Gwen Hernandez

Gwen Hernandez is the author of the romantic suspense series *Men of Steele* and the nonfiction book *Productivity Tools for Writers*. Before becoming a professional writer, Gwen worked in computer programming and was also an engineer.

A friend recommended Scrivener to her not long after she began writing and at first she was skeptical. "I remember thinking, *why on earth would I need writing software?* I have a word processor—I was using Word—and I couldn't imagine what it could possibly bring to the table. But pretty much instantly I realized the value," she says. Her first reaction was "amazement" and once she started using Scrivener she discovered many features that would enhance her writing process. "The fact that it would open up to where I left off was brilliant in my mind, and the ability to see the whole structure of your story and shuffle things around as needed, go immediately where you need to go, color-code things to keep yourself on track, leave notes for yourself—everything. It just blew me away."

Gwen's writing process is completely different for her fiction and nonfiction, and Scrivener easily adapts to this. "It's nice having a program that supports both styles," she says. Her fiction style is based around the four-part story structure—a modification of the three-part—and she begins in Scrivener by creating four "part" folders in the binder, and creating her scenes in there. "When I start it's just part folders with lots of scene documents in them. I don't think in chapters so much as I think in scenes. I organize into chapters after I've got the whole first draft written and feel pretty solid with it." For her fiction she doesn't outline in great detail and is more of a "pantser" when it comes to plotting. Scrivener helps her to feel organized and see the structure of her story clearly. "Even though my process is very disorganized, Scrivener helps me keep it all together," she says.

When writing nonfiction her approach is very different, and she carefully outlines and creates folders for each chapter. "Being able to use the color-coding to keep track of where I was in the process for each individual chapter, and what I needed to work on next, was invaluable."

During the drafting process Gwen writes in the full-screen composition mode to block out distractions and uses project targets to help stay motivated. For fiction, she writes each scene based on a brief outline on a synopsis card, and then uses color-coding to keep track of which character's point of view she is in. Gwen uses annotations and comments while writing to flag issues to check, fix or research later.

For self-editing she also uses color-coding to keep track of where she is in the process. She reads her first draft on her iPad and listens to her book through Scrivener's text-to-speech function as an added way of picking up any errors that have slipped through. Her editors and beta readers edit in Word documents using Track Changes, so she uses two monitors and manually takes her changes back into Scrivener.

When it comes to formatting her books and teaching others about the Compile feature, Gwen has found it can take time for most people to understand that it is based on a "rules oriented" instead of a "what you see is what you get oriented" output process. "If you've used Word your whole life and you are not a software programmer it's really weird. Because every word processor out there is WYSIWYG (What You See Is What You Get). It's taken me until recently to think of it as applying rules to types and really making sure people understand the hierarchy of the binder and what that means. Because if you can get the levels down then you can understand the formatting tab and compile—and you've got it nailed." She has found that some people become frustrated when trying to use Scrivener to create a publishing layout, and explains, "It's invented as a drafting tool. The fact that you can self-publish in it—bonus. It's not meant to be layout software: it's writing software."

Gwen uses Scrivener for blogging, saying: "It serves as an archive of all of my blog posts. Fully searchable, organized by year, month, etc. and color-coded by which blog website it's on." Another unique way she uses Scrivener is for project management. She has set up an "appearances project" and uses folders within to collate, track and archive all the workshops, courses and appearances she does for others. "Anytime I'm going to give a workshop or an online course or a guest blog or some kind of interview—I have all of the information there." In Scrivener, everything is searchable which helps when planning future appearances. "I don't have to recreate the wheel every single time I give a workshop," she says.

You can find more about her books on Gwen's website at www.gwenhernandez.com.

Watch the full interview on YouTube.[5]

Joe Bunting

Joe Bunting is the author of *Let's Write a Short Story* and founder of the blog The Write Practice. Both his book and blog show authors how to be become productive and successful creative writers through daily practice of their craft.

Joe is also a ghostwriter, and he wrote his first book in 2010. "I was using Microsoft Word and one thing about working on a big file like a book, it just becomes unmanageable. It takes like five minutes to load and it's just a big pain. I discovered Scrivener on my second book and it made everything much easier," he says.

While Joe has encountered some authors who are resistant to trying Scrivener—as it can seem overwhelming—he was interested in trying it. "Personally I was really, really excited about it and felt like it was a huge motivator."

Writing in Scrivener also helped him to write more freely. "When I was using Microsoft Word I found myself just putting everything into one document and having to write chronologically, because that's how it works. One of the nice things about Scrivener that I soon found really helpful is that I could jump around a lot easier, as my writing led me, and just use it as a place for capture. I could free write about whatever I wanted to write about that day and put it in a folder, and I knew that folder was eventually going to be a chapter. It allowed me to be more spontaneous and creative because I had more flexibility."

When ghostwriting nonfiction books for clients, a lot of the content is provided and Joe uses Scrivener for structuring and editing. "Mostly what I do is I organize and rewrite and Scrivener makes that just so much easier."

Joe sees the strengths and weaknesses of a range of writing

tools, and uses different tools for different purposes. "I use Evernote for capturing research and Scrivener for composing and capturing my own writing. Usually I will use Scrivener for composing the first and maybe second draft, then for editing I often switch to Microsoft Word." For exporting to ePub files Joe uses Word, Scrivener, or Pages, and then Sigil to edit directly in the ePub file. "Sigil is an ePub editor that I definitely recommend if you're working with ebooks," he says.

Although not exclusively using Scrivener for the entire writing process, Joe is more than happy with all it does. "There is no other tool that is as great as Scrivener for structuring your book, for organizing things, for managing large documents, even documents like book proposals or long articles. It's not just for books. For managing those large projects, it's perfect, but it's not perfect for everything. Could it be perfect for everything? Maybe. But maybe you can't make it perfect without breaking it," he says. For more on writing craft, visit Joe's blog at www.thewritepractice.com.

Watch the full interview on YouTube.[6]

Rachel Aaron

Rachel Aaron is a fantasy and science fiction author who has been writing full-time since 2009. *The Legend of Eli Monpress* and *The Paradox Trilogy* (as Rachel Bach) are both published by  Orbit, and she has recently self-published the first two books in *The Heartstrikers Series* plus the nonfiction book *2,000 to 10,000: How to Write Faster, Write Better, and Write More of What You Love*. The latter describes how she went from writing 2,000 words a day to 10,000 words a day without increasing her writing time, and it has been a big hit, helping many fellow writers transform their process and become more productive.

Hearing about Scrivener shortly after discovering her 2k to 10k method, Rachel was thrilled to find a program so intuitively suited to her needs. "I was still writing in Word back then because apparently I lived in the Stone Age. But I started the fifth (*Eli Monpress*) book with my process *and* Scrivener—and that was like writing candy. It was smooth. It immediately clicked," she says.

Prior to becoming a full-time author she was a web developer and is analytical in her approach to writing. "There are many different ways of thinking about plots—but I like to think about mine as a system. We have a problem. We have characters. We have all these different things that are all going on at the same time and somehow they all have to make sense. They all have to happen together. And they all have to happen in a way that is interesting. And that's a pretty big challenge." Scrivener excels in managing this challenge and allows Rachel to track the unique information relating to the characters and world she is currently writing in—and to keep it all in one place. "That is one of the things I love about Scrivener. I can just make a folder, I can name it anything, I can throw as many pages or pictures or links to other things as I want under there and just keep track of it all."

For her fiction books she outlines heavily, and prefers to do this in longhand to begin with. But once she is ready to go into detail, everything goes into Scrivener. Rachel has created her own Scrivener template, which includes a title page, a chapter page and a resources section. "In the resource section I always have: plot, characters, world, cuts, a folder called edits and an individual page called worksheet, which is where I keep track of all my writing times and numbers. Because for every book I write I'm going to have a plot, I'm going to have characters and I'm going to have a world; I'm going to cut stuff out of it and I'm going to have edits. And then I just change these as I go."

When plotting she creates a document called her "scene diagram," a list of where each scene fits and a basic one-sentence description of what's happening in that scene. "I use the scene diagram when I'm looking at my novel to remind me of where I am and what's going to happen next," Rachel says. Using the split screen mode to view her scene diagram and her novel at the same time makes this process seamless. A lover of lists, she also creates them for her timeline, scene map and editing notes, all of which play important roles during the drafting and editing stages.

Rachel is aware that she only uses a small number of the available features in Scrivener, but keeping it simple works for her. She sticks to using her template and her lists and loves being able to create infinite folders for chapters and resources. The word count feature is also huge and she customizes things to suit her individual preferences and process. "Scrivener is my environment as a writer. It's very nice; I feel like it's my workspace," she says.

Rachel's blog is full of tips on becoming a more productive and professional writer and can be found—along with all her books—on her website at www.rachelaaron.net.

Watch the full interview on YouTube.[7]

Simon Whistler

Author and voice talent Simon Whistler is perhaps best known for his weekly podcast, *Rocking Self-Publishing*, which features interviews with indie authors and covers a broad range of themes and topics relevant to writers looking to self-publish their work. Following the success of his podcast he published two books in the "For Indies" series, *Audiobooks for Indies* and *Bootstrapping for Indies*, that aim to share his knowledge with a broader audience.

He first encountered Scrivener during his podcast interviews when different authors mentioned how it had transformed their writing process. He decided to try it for himself and discovered that the Binder and other tools for organizing made writing his books so much easier.

Before Scrivener, he used Google Docs for his writing. "I had like 20,000 words tapped out in there which was simple to do but became confusing. I basically just couldn't manage that, just having to search through to find things. Making the transition from Google Docs to Scrivener was also a no-brainer, and I'd been told Scrivener does the organization of things through those files and folders you get on the left hand side. Basically, I grabbed everything from the Doc file and dropped it into Scrivener," Simon says. From here he was able to sort out chapters, so he could easily find topics that he wanted to expand on to finish the book.

Simon's process involves setting up text files and giving them each a title relating to a subject he wants to cover within his book. "Then I go through and I use the synopsis bit to put some notes on what I want to cover. Basically when the writing process actually happens, then I finally go into the main text edit bit in the center.

I go through and expand on each of these points very quickly, and then those get crafted into the final book."

Simon admits he is not one to sit through the tutorials, preferring to learn as he goes. He uses the Targets feature to keep to him on track with deadlines, and likes the option of the split screen mode. His self-editing process consists of a number of drafts. "I'll definitely do the very rough ideas draft, taking those notes in the synopsis and document notes section and writing from that. Then I would say the next thing I do is still a draft. The next thing after that is still a draft and then maybe I start editing." His editing involves mostly checking the order and structure, leaving the job of spotting typos and fixing grammar to an editor. He also uses the text-to-speech function that is built into Scrivener to listen to his book, as it helps him notice errors that he may have missed when reading.

While researching his next book, *Productivity for Indies*, Simon asked various authors to share their productivity hacks. "Scrivener gets an unfair number of mentions," he says. Simon's weekly podcast and archived author interviews can be found at www.rockingselfpublishing.com.

Watch the full interview on YouTube.[8]

PART 3

For Mac

How to Write a Story in Scrivener

A Walkthrough of Scrivener's User Interface

In the Scrivener walkthroughs and workshops I've done, one of the most common complaints from new users is that the interface is confusing and overwhelming. People find it difficult to get used to new software, so they give up before they even get started.

Don't worry. I'm going to walk you through the important pieces of Scrivener's interface, their names, and what each one is used for right now.

First, Install Scrivener

In order to get the most out of this book, download and install Scrivener on your computer and follow along as we explore the program.[9]

Take advantage of the thirty-day free trial or buy the program for a one-time fee of $45.

Windows Versus Mac

One more note before we get to the walkthrough: For the most part, the functionality of Scrivener for Mac and Scrivener for Windows is comparable, but there are a few notable differences. This is the Mac tutorial, and uses screenshots on the Mac OS X operating system.

If you're on a Windows PC, jump over to the Windows version of the tutorial.

Project Templates

Now, let's get started!

The first screen you'll see when you open Scrivener is Project Templates. From here, you can create a blank project, start a project based on an existing template, or open a recent project.

For now, open a blank project to follow along. I'll talk more about templates and teach you how to create your own when I introduce my No Nonsense Novel Template later on.

Blank Project

This is what a blank new project in Scrivener looks like. You'll see an identical screen if you are following along.

Menu

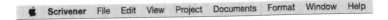

The Menu is where you can find a full list of actions and functions, whether that's adding links and images to documents, printing, compiling, formatting, etc.

I like to spend some time with any new piece of software familiarizing myself with the Menus because they're *always* different, and always very powerful.

Don't just look at the actions, but try to perform each one. If you can't figure out what an action does, there's a handy (but dense) Scrivener Manual which you can search. Find this by going to **Help > Scrivener Manual** in the Menu.

Binder

The Binder is the left-most area of the interface. Its job is to contain all of the documents and folders in your project.

While most new projects give you a basic Binder structure to start with, it is completely customizable. The structure pictured above is what you will see if you open a new project using the novel template that comes with Scrivener.

The Binder is one of Scrivener's greatest advantages over other word processing software because it allows you to quickly and easily jump between sections of your manuscript, research, and other folders with scene-level granularity.

Toolbar

The Toolbar is the gray bar across the top of the program where common actions are located.

The screenshot above is the default configuration on Mac, but you can customize the Toolbar by adding and removing buttons. Simply right click and select **Customize Toolbar...** to check out the additional buttons and options.

Inspector

The Inspector is the menu on the right hand side. Open and close it by clicking the Inspector button (the blue "i" in the circle) at the top right of the default Toolbar.

Within the Inspector, you can switch between several panes using the buttons at the top of the Inspector area. From left to right, these panes are named:

- Notes
- References
- Keywords
- Custom Meta-Data
- Snapshots
- Comments & Footnotes

In Notes, the first pane, I use everything. I use the Synopsis pane to write a summary of the scene I'm working on, the Labels and Status to label and set the status of each file of a draft. I also use the Document Notes section to take notes while I'm writing, as a kind of scene-specific scratch pad. Each document you create in Scrivener has a Synopsis and Notes section as pictured above.

Then we have the Snapshots pane. This is a crucial tool for me during the revision process. I take snapshots at the end of each draft so that I have rollback points saved in case I screw something up, change my mind, or dislike the edits I made for whatever reason.

Finally, here's a screenshot of the Comments pane. This is for leaving comments within your manuscript. To insert a comment, use the **Format** > **Comment** action in the Menu, click the Comment button in the Toolbar, or use the shortcut **Command+Shift+***.

Explore the other panes, Custom Meta-Data, and Keywords if you want to, but don't worry about them too much. Personally, I rarely use them.

Editor

The Editor is the important part in the middle, the blank page that you write in. This is where you make sentences and create your stories, and where you'll be spending most of your time.

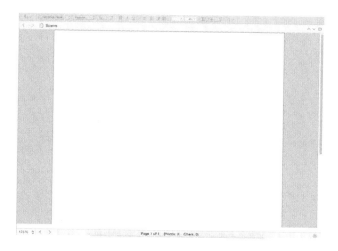

The Editor can be full screen, or swapped to Page View like I have it above. I like Page View because it shows the gutters at both sides of the page, which feels cleaner to me. You can toggle Page View on or off by going to **View > Page View > Show/Hide Page View** in the Menu.

There are other view options as well, such as showing a Ruler at the top of the editor so you can adjust tabs and margins. Do whatever makes you happy. Play around with it! The Editor, too, is completely customizable, so you can make the background bright pink if you want to.

Group/View Mode

Depending on where you are, these three buttons in the toolbar will be labeled "Group Mode" (when viewing a group of documents) or "View Mode" (when viewing an individual document).

They allow you to seamlessly switch between seeing your documents and subdocuments in the Editor. From left to right they are called Scrivenings ("View the document/group of documents"), Corkboard ("View the document's subdocuments on the corkboard"), or Outliner ("View the document's subdocuments in the outliner") viewing modes.

These are the most powerful buttons in Scrivener because they allow you to toggle between perspectives of your manuscript, another one of Scrivener's big advantages over linear, single-column word processing programs.

Scrivenings

Use the Group/View Mode button on the left to get to the Scrivenings view. This is your default view.

If you click on a single document in the Binder in this view, you'll be shown the text in that document within the Editor.

If you click on a folder, you'll be shown the text of all files within that folder in order, with marks delineating where one file ends and another begins.

In the screenshot above, I've also turned on an option to show the title of a file while in the Scrivenings view. You can toggle this convenient option on and off in the Menu by going to **Format > Options > Show Titles in Scrivenings**.

Corkboard

The middle Group/View Mode button brings up the Corkboard view.

The Corkboard is used to simulate the experience of a real-life corkboard. You can organize and edit multiple documents using a card-based interface. Snap the cards to a grid or move them around freely (depending on your settings). The size of the cards can also be changed. While it doesn't have the infinite flexibility of a real-life corkboard, I find that the digital Corkboard is faster to use, especially if you're making large structural changes.

You might outline a story using the notecards, rearrange the order of scenes by dragging and dropping them, or view all of your sketches in one place for a high-level overview. Fill the front of the index cards with text, or replace the text with an image.

Outliner

The last Group/View Mode button brings you to the Outliner, which allows you to see all your documents and metadata in a structured list.

View your entire manuscript in the Outliner, or drill down into a specific folder for a narrower view.

The columns and data you see in the screenshot above are completely customizable. Add or remove columns by right clicking on the column headers (or clicking on the arrow to the right of the column headings) and selecting the new column you'd like to add from the list that appears. You can also find these options under the Menu by going to **View > Outliner Columns** in the Menu.

That concludes our tour! Are you feeling a little better now? I hope learning the vocabulary and seeing the interface broken down into its component parts makes you feel more comfortable in the program. There's a lot to get used to for a new user, so I suggest taking a little time to explore the interface on your own. Get acquainted with the Binder and the Toolbar, especially, so that you can follow along in the next chapters.

How to Structure Your Story

Why Structure Matters

In the blank project you created to follow along during the walkthrough, direct your attention to the Binder on the left hand side. Here you'll create and organize your story and all material related to its development, such as sketches, outlines, research, drafts, and anything else you wish to keep track of.

The Binder is one of the primary advantages of using Scrivener, and it's the feature that convinces many writers to make the transition to the program from other writing software. The Binder is your writing desk. It allows you to keep all of your work in one place, stay organized with folders and subfolders, and access your work quickly when you need it.

Bird's-Eye View

Another benefit of the Binder is that it gives you a bird's-eye view of y our story.

Most word processors don't have a feature that supplies this kind of visual. Instead, a writer must resort to drawing the story structure by hand, stacking sticky notes or index cards, or using a spreadsheet to lay it out. If the structure changes, as it often does while drafting, extra work must be done to maintain that diagram. Scrivener automates this process with the Binder. If you break down your manuscript correctly (which we'll cover in a moment), you'll be able to visualize the story with a glance at the Binder. Scenes will be nested into chapters and chapters into parts, according to how your story is structured.

A bird's-eye view of structure in the Binder empowers you to spot structural issues early on. Once you know your story, you'll be able to tell where the key moments are (inciting incident, first plot point, climax, resolution, etc.) and whether they fall in the right place to ensure genre-appropriate pacing. If part two of your book seems sluggish, you might look at your Binder and notice that there are significantly more scenes in part two than there are in part one, part three, or part four. Other obvious storytelling problems such as a climax that comes too early or a resolution that drags on too long are also apparent once you know what to look for in the Binder.

To give a specific example, when I finished the rough draft of my first novel I got some editorial feedback indicating in no uncertain terms that my male point-of-view character had an incomplete story. Sure enough, when I analyzed my draft in the Binder, he had fewer scenes and fewer chapters than my female point-of-view character. I hadn't realized this obvious issue while I was writing the draft, but my readers did. And there it was, plain as day, in the Binder. If I had been using a traditional word processor with no Binder, it would have been much harder to accept. With the visual in front of me, it was easy to evaluate the criticism objectively and take steps to fix the problem.

Required Folders in the Binder

There are three required folders in every Scrivener project.

1. The **Draft** or **Manuscript** folder, which contains all of the chapters and scenes that comprise your story. Consider anything in this folder officially "on the page." Everything you type in there will be Compiled in the final book file by default.

2. The **Research** folder is one of an unlimited number of containers where you store project-related information.

Nothing in this folder (or any other folder) goes into the final book file by default.

3. The **Trash** is where files go when you delete them. You can empty the trash if you wish to remove these files permanently. Once you empty the trash, there's no undo button.

You can't delete these folders, but you may rename them.

The Binder Is Yours to Command

While a default research folder is included in every Scrivener project, there's no requirement to stuff all your work in there. Create as many new folders and files as you need and organize them however you please.

I like to have separate folders for Research, Characters and Settings at the very least. I invariably add new folders as the need arises. Here are some examples of other folders I keep in my Binder: cut scenes, old drafts, sales copy and keywords, brainstorming lists, to-do lists, front matter, series arcs, freewriting, ideas, etc.

I've done enough work in Scrivener that I like to start with a set of common folders. You can see what that looks like for me by checking out my No Nonsense Novel Template.

How to Structure Your Manuscript Folder

There's no right or wrong way to structure your research and development folders. There are, however, best practices when it comes to structuring your Manuscript folder.

To get a firm grasp on how Scrivener is supposed to be structured, we have to go back to a basic structural principle of storytelling.

Scenes Are the Basic Unit of Storytelling

Veteran editor and writer Shawn Coyne, author of *The Story Grid: What Good Editors Know*, writes that the basic unit of storytelling is the scene: "While it can be broken down into its component beats, the scene is the most obvious mini-story."

Scrivener is also designed using the concept of the scene as the basic unit of storytelling. The program works best when you break your stories out so that each scene is in its own file, and those scenes are arranged into sections/chapter folders which roll up into part folders. That way, when you're ready to compile, your Manuscript folder is already structured to take full advantage of the Compiler.

How to Structure a Novel

Many novels abide by a simple structure. A number of chapters containing one or more scenes are arranged in order. If your story is using this simple novel structure, your Manuscript folder will be arranged like this:

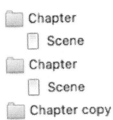

The way you title your chapter folders will be important during the final Compile process. For instance, you can tell the Compiler to name your chapters based on what you titled your chapter folders. Traditionally, the titles of scenes are left out, so you can simply number them. However, I name them with a simple sentence, like "hero meets villain," so that I know what they contain. You'll thank yourself for naming your scenes later if you end up moving them around while you're revising.

How to Structure a Novel with Parts

A more complex novel will follow the simple novel structure, except those chapters will be arranged into larger containers called parts. If you are writing a novel with parts, use this structure.

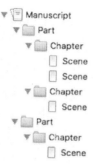

Again, as a best practice, name your part and chapter folders how you want them to appear in the final book file. You can number the chapters automatically during the Compile process, or choose to use or not use the names of the chapters, parts, and scenes according to your needs. Naming them now will make it easier for you to navigate your book during the writing process.

How to Structure a Nonfiction Manuscript with Parts

A nonfiction manuscript with parts is similar to a novel with parts. Here's an example of a nonfiction manuscript generated using the Non-Fiction (with Parts) template that comes packaged with Scrivener.

```
▼ 📄 Manuscript
    📄 Title Page
    📄 Contents
    📄 Foreword
    ▼ 📁 Chapter Subtitle
        ▼ 📄 Section
            📄 Sub-Section
        ▼ 📄 Section
            📄 Sub-Section
    ▼ 📁 Chapter Subtitle
        ▼ 📄 Section
            📄 Sub-Section
    📄 Endnotes
```

In this example, there are several documents that appear in the manuscript before the first chapter begins, and an endnotes file as well. If your book is structured like this, check out the Non-Fiction (with Parts) template to get you started.

How This Book Is Structured

Like the previous example, the book you're reading is a nonfiction book with multiple parts.

Here's how the first couple parts of this book appear in the Binder:

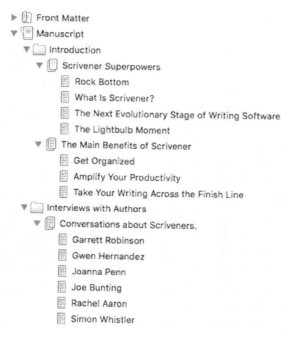

Notice how the nesting dictates where the parts are, where the subheadings are, and where the sections are. Unlike a novel, where I use only the chapter names, for nonfiction books I rely on the names of the documents to generate the subheadings in the final book file.

Where to Put Front and Back Matter

In the screenshot above you'll also see that I have a Front Matter folder.

Front matter is anything that comes before the beginning of your story: a title page, copyright, table of contents, etc. Front matter goes in a separate folder outside the Manuscript folder. Many templates generate front matter templates for you, so I'd recommend opening a few new projects using the templates Scrivener provides and checking them out. During the Compile process (which we'll cover in detail in a later chapter) you can choose which folder/file to use as the front matter for your compiled book.

Back matter is a bit different. To have files appear at the end of your manuscript, like calls-to-action, teasers of your next book, and your author bio, you have to place those folders inside the Manuscript folder after the last chapter of your book, as if they were any other chapter. There's no place in the Compile process to select what to include as your back matter.

Structure Smart

Break your story down by scene, arrange those scenes into their containing chapters and those chapters into their containing parts, and you'll be prepared for revisions and the Compiling process later. Not only that, but you'll automate the diagramming of your story structure and be able to spot problems with your manuscript early.

How to Create Character Sketches

How do you create compelling characters?

Nothing is born in a vacuum. Characters don't emerge fully formed. Creating compelling characters is a process of getting to know them and working to make them come to life. They're developed through character sketches, through the writing process itself, through lots feedback, and through diligent revision.

What Is a Character Sketch?

Think of a character sketch as the rough draft of your character. It's a place where you can freely experiment, where you can tell yourself who your characters are, how they look, and where they come from.

You can type out their whole backstory or just the parts of the timeline that inform your character's identity. Their inner and external conflicts will be crucial to your story, so be sure to include those, too.

Most importantly, use character sketches as a tool to discover your characters' key motivations and goals, because they are the engine that drives your story forward.

How to Use Template Sheets in Scrivener

Scrivener has Template Sheets that make building out character sketches easy. If you started using one of their document templates, like the novel template that comes with Scrivener or my No Nonsense Novel Template, there should already be a Template Sheets folder in the your project document that looks like this screenshot:

If not, you can make a Template Sheets folder by creating a new folder in the Binder, selecting it, and then from the Menu choosing **Project > Set Selection as Templates Folder**.

Visualize Your Characters Using Scrivener's Corkboard

Now that you have your Template Sheets folder set up, you can generate character sketches by creating new files from the Template Sheets you've created.

There are two ways to do this. In the Toolbar, click and hold the Add button, go to **New From Template,** and then click on the template you wish to create. Or, right click on the folder you wish to add a new sketch to in the Binder, then go to **Add > New From Template > Name of Your Template**.

Here's the cast of characters from an early draft of my first novel:

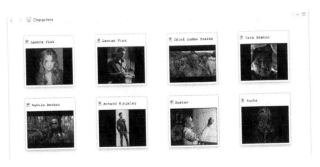

I go for visuals out of the gate, as it helps me ground my character in an image. Having a photo in front of me makes writing about them easier, at first, because the photos jog my imagination. Once I really know my characters (i.e. about twenty-five percent of the way through the first draft), I don't need to look at the visuals at all. By that point I have a more vivid image of the characters in my head.

If you can't find photos for every character, that's okay. Remember that nothing about your planning or pre-production phase (to borrow a film term) is set in stone. Your story will evolve as you write, and so will your characters.

For the images, I've picked a few photos I found online.

There are several excellent resources on the Internet to get free stock photos. Here are some of my favorites:

- Unsplash
- Wikimedia Commons
- Pexels
- Pixabay
- MorgueFile[10]

To add a photo to a Character Sketch in Scrivener, open your character's notecard and find the Notes pane of the Inspector. Change the Synopsis pane to take an image by using the switcher in the top right of the Synopsis frame (the little orange graphic with double arrows next to it in the screenshot below), then drag your image into the black image area where you can see the phrase "Drag in an image file":

To insert a photo inline with the text of your sketch, first click where you want the photo, and then go to **Edit > Insert > Image from File...**

You can also drag and drop photos into the Editor to accomplish the same task.

Individual Character Sketches

Here's a screenshot of an individual sketch of one of my characters:

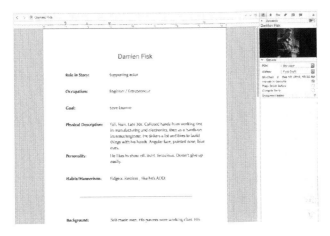

This sketch was created using the Character Sketch Template Sheet that comes with Scrivener. I've since abandoned Scrivener's defaults in favor of my own compilation, which follows.

An Alternative Character Sketch Template

As you learn more about character sketches, you'll probably want to customize your character sketch template and make it your own. Personally, I find Scrivener's default sketch sheets superficial. When sketching characters, I like less structure and fewer prescriptive fields concerning the character's physical appearance and personality.

This is my preferred character sketch, the same one I include in my No Nonsense Novel Template. Here's what it looks like in Scrivener:

And here's the full text, which you can feel free to use or modify as you see fit:

[character photo]

FULL NAME

One Sentence Synopsis
This character in a single sentence.

Summary
This is a paragraph summary of your character. Include

physical attributes, habits, mannerisms. Sketch your character.

Motivations & Goals
What do they want?

Conflicts
What makes them human?

Narrative
What happens to them in the story? What else is important?

Why Character Sketches Work

There are practical reasons to do character sketches. For one, developing characters is a process. Starting with character sketches is a great way to give the gel of your ideas time and space to set.

Yes, they're extra effort, and yes, they can be difficult. But that's part of the process.

If you feel like you really know the character and are ready to move on, run through this checklist to double check your work:

1. What is your character's primary motivation?
2. How does your character change through the cours the story?
3. What does your character look like?
4. How does your character act around their parents? Their friends? Their boss?
5. How does your character respond under stress?
6. What is your character's weakness, their kryptonite?
7. What will your character die for?
8. What is your character's biggest hypocrisy?
9. Who are your character's friends?

If you can answer all of these questions with confidence, congratulations, you're ready for setting sketches, which are covered in the next section.

How to Create Setting Sketches

"If character is the foreground of fiction, setting is the background," Janet Burroway tells the reader in *Writing Fiction: A Guide to Narrative Craft*. But how do you create engaging settings that enhance your story? And how can Scrivener help you create setting sketches for your particular story?

People (and therefore characters) are a product of their environment, for good or for ill. In order to write compelling stories that draw readers in, you not only have to know your setting intimately, but be able to manipulate that setting to bring out the best and worst in your characters.

A good setting can take on personality traits of its own, and some tend to think of setting as another character.[11]

All settings have to start somewhere. Let's go over a classic method to help you flesh out your settings early in the process so that they can become a vital part of your story.

What Is a Setting Sketch?

A setting sketch is an outline of a fictional place—what it looks like, smells like, feels like. You can discuss a setting objectively through the lens of your own experiences, or you can take the same setting and examine it through the eyes of a character.

Settings also create atmosphere and tone in your story. Horror stories are great examples of effective setting because they create an atmosphere of fear that is almost palpable; it's what makes them such gripping stories, whether you're working with a haunted house, a zombie apocalypse, or a ruined castle.

As with character sketches, I like to start with visuals using Scrivener's Corkboard.

Character or Setting Sketch—Which Comes First?

In the last chapter, we talked about how character sketches can help you flesh out the characters in your story, so you might be wondering: Which should you work on first, your character sketches or your setting sketches?

Both character and setting sketches are fundamental to the planning phase of the creative writing process, but the order in which you tackle them is your choice.

I'm of the mindset that you can do setting, character, or plot in any order that makes the most sense to you. Play to your own strengths.

Don't worry too much about what you do first. Over time, you will develop your own process, and adjust these tactics and tools to fit your style.

Using Template Sheets in Scrivener for Setting Sketches

As with character sketches, you'll want to use the Template Sheets for setting sketches.

Visualize Your Settings

Start by creating a folder called "Settings." Then open that folder to the Corkboard view and create a notecard for each setting in your story using Template Sheets, the same way we did for character sketches in the last chapter. As a reminder, you can either right click on the folder and go to **Add > New From Template** and select your setting sketch, or click and hold on the **Add** button in the Toolbar to add new sketches.

If your whole story takes place in one room in one house, you might have only a single card. More likely though, your story takes place in multiple settings.

Try to be as specific as possible. Instead of "New York City," name your card "The Village" or, even better, "Italian Restaurant in the Village." The more specific your setting, the more likely it is to come to life.

Once you have all your setting notecards arranged, go find one image that feels like it matches each setting. There can be discrepancies between the details of the photo you choose and the actual setting in your story. The idea isn't to find a photo that represents your story in every way possible, but to capture the spirit of that particular setting so you have a place to start your sketch.

Here are the setting cards I created for my novel:

If you find it necessary to use more than one photo, you can add extra images inside the Scrivenings view of a particular sketch.

Write About Your Setting

Now for the fun part: open up a setting and start writing.

Here's a screenshot of what the default Template Sheet for a setting sketch looks like in Scrivener. I've filled it out with one of the settings in my novel.

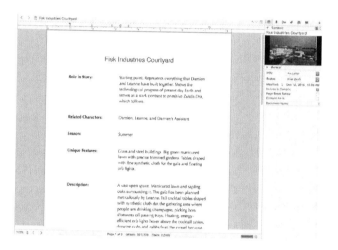

Aim for at least 500 words. Any more than that is icing on the cake. Any less than that and you may find yourself coming back to the sketch to flesh it out more as you write. Better to have it and not need it than the other way around.

SCRIVENER SUPERPOWERS

An Alternative Setting Sketch Template

Here's an alternative setting sketch template you may use in your writing practice. This is my preferred setting sketch.

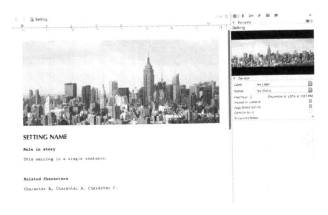

What I like about this version, compared to Scrivener's default, is that it's less prescriptive. It leaves room for the imagination to run wild, cuing you with suggestions rather than specific questions. For example, you see in the default sketch above, the label "season"? All I wrote there was "summer." That wasn't important to my story, so it was really just a waste of a label. In my sketch, I've combined "Weather & Seasons," as I find that there is a lot of information to mine with both those categories, whereas a season alone isn't very significant in the stories I want to tell.

You have plenty of room to experiment here, so mix and match until you find what works for you.

Here's the full text of my setting sketch. Feel free to use or modify it as you see fit:

[setting photo]

SETTING NAME

Role in Story
This setting in a single sentence.

Related Characters
Character A, Character B, Character C.

Description
Describe your setting in significant detail.

Weather & Season
Windy, rainy, gloomy, sunny, clear, foggy, humid, altitude, storms?
Summer, spring, fall, winter?

Sights, Sounds & Smells
Use your senses and go there. Sketch out what aspects of your setting are most important to your character, what they look like, smell like, how the characters feel when they see this place.

Details
Anything else important to remember?

Setting Sketch Checklist

How do you know when your setting sketch is done? That depends on your own unique process. You're done when you can't squeeze any more juice out of the setting you're working on.

Just in case you're still not sure, here's a checklist you can run through that may help you out. Consider each of your setting sketches and ask yourself the following questions:

1. What unique atmosphere does this setting evoke?

2. What important role does this setting play in my story?

3. Would my story be the same if I changed this setting? Why or why not?

4. Go through the weather patterns: rain, wind, snow, hot, cold, humid—what about this setting is consistent in each type of weather? What about this setting is inconsistent?
5. What year is it in this setting? Why does that matter?
6. How does this setting influence each of my characters?

How to Storyboard Your Story

Storyboarding is the process of mapping out your story, often using index cards, in a high-level way that allows you to see your story visually and rearrange it.

Scrivener's Corkboard provides the perfect interface to storyboard your novel digitally.

When Should You Storyboard?

The storyboarding process can be undertaken at any phase in the writing of a story. Storyboarding is a tool I use several times during the writing process: before I begin writing (i.e. planning/plotting), during the rough draft (when I get stuck), and when I'm revising. It's a way to see the big picture, make sure your story has good bones and ensure that everything flows logically from one scene to the next.

It's also the tool that allows you to combine the work you've done for the previous three chapters: your knowledge of how to structure your manuscript, your characters, and your settings. Your storyboard is where they all come together. Having characters, settings, and an idea of your plot in mind ahead of time will make the storyboarding process much simpler.

SCRIVENER SUPERPOWERS

How to Create Your Storyboard in Scrivener

Follow these steps to storyboard in Scrivener:

1. **To Begin, Create a New Folder.**
   Move the new folder outside of the Manuscript section of the Binder. Call this folder "Storyboard."

2. **View the Folder as a Corkboard.**
   After you create your new storyboarding folder, open it, and view it as a Corkboard (background color/style varies depending on your settings):

   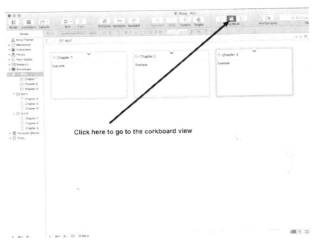

3. **Create Index Cards for the Major Sections of Your Book.**
   Next, create an index card for your first act or chapter. To do this, just create a new document, as you normally would for a new scene, within the Storyboard folder. When you use the Corkboard view, these documents will be shown as index cards.

   I'll let you start as big as you want. Sometimes, I'll start planning (especially in the early phase of idea generation) with only three or four cards, one for each "act." Sometimes I start with a "beginning" card and an "end" card.

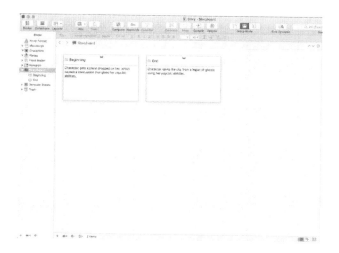

There's no right or wrong way.

Let's say you've thought about it for a while and have a vague idea of how your chapters should be laid out. Great. Create a card and write the title of the chapter at the top of the card.

Even if you don't plan to title your chapters in the final story, use titles as an exercise in specificity. Maybe you're writing a literary story and you want those fancy roman numerals to head each chapter, or you don't want chapter breaks at all, just a blank space between sections like Frank McCourt uses in *Angela's Ashes*. That's fine. Challenge yourself to title your sections anyway. This isn't the final result, but an exercise in getting to know your story better.

In the body of the card, write a one or two sentence description of the main purpose of the chapter, like I've done in the screenshot above. The goal here is to get to the point. Often, I don't know what the main purpose of my chapter is and I'll have to think really hard about it. Sometimes I delete a chapter entirely.

Other times I break a chapter into two because there are two important points I want to hit. In both cases, the story is stronger for it.

Once you're done with the first chapter card, create a new index card for the second, third, fourth, etc. until you've reached the end of your story. It's that simple, but unless you're an experienced storyteller—and perhaps even if you are—it won't be easy.

4. **Create Index Cards for Each Scene.**
Once your first round of cards is complete, it's time to go deeper into your story. If you started with acts, break them down into scenes.

Challenge yourself to be as specific as possible. Scenes are the basic unit of storytelling,[12] as we've discussed, so your goal is to get down to the scene level.

If you write those short one-scene chapters like Dan Brown or David Baldacci, you're in luck: that's as deep as you need to go. Keep in mind that not everyone writes that way. Often, books have multiple scenes within each chapter, so keep breaking your index cards down until you have a card for each scene.

At this point, you might have to make an organizational decision. You can nest your scenes within your chapters (or your chapters within your acts), which will require a lot of hopping up and down levels to view the cards you've created across the whole story, but which will show fewer cards on the screen at any given time. Or you can keep them all on one screen. Here's an example three-act story structure with three chapters in each act, opened to Act I. As you can see, when you're viewing Act I, you're limited to seeing just the cards within the selected folder.

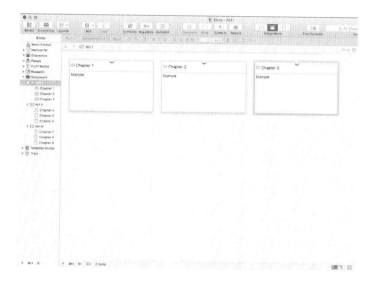

If you're writing an epic fantasy novel, I would understand if you wanted to nest your chapters and scenes within larger containers like this. Storyboard one act at a time to make it less overwhelming.

Next, when we transition to a physical medium, you'll be able to get a big picture view.

5. **Print Out Your Storyboard.**
   You would need several screens to get a good bird's-eye view of your story on the computer. Fortunately, now that you've begun to storyboard in Scrivener, you can transition to a physical version very easily. All you need is a printer and a pair of scissors.

   While you're in the Corkboard view, go to **File > Print Current Document...** and print out the digital notecards you've created. Scrivener will print these with dotted borders around each card.

Now, it's arts and crafts day in school! Grab a pair of scissors and cut the paper into individual index cards. Then use an actual corkboard with pushpins—or the floor, or a long piece of butcher paper—to lay it all out.

I used this process when I was rewriting *The Auriga Project*. Here's what my story looks like on a physical corkboard. Each card is a scene, and each group of cards represents a chapter.

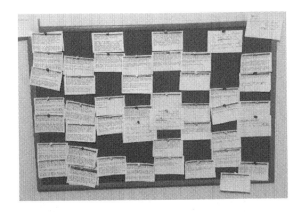

One note of warning: if your description within the body of the index card in Scrivener is too long, the text will overflow to multiple cards when you print it out. If that happens, pare back your description or simply stack the cards after you cut them out.

This step isn't strictly necessary. I don't usually print out my storyboard until I'm on my second or third draft and I need a way to see the story with fresh eyes. Again, you'll develop your own process. Do what's best for you.

Corkboard Settings

This is a good time to point out some Corkboard settings. Using the button in the bottom right of the Corkboard interface, you can change the size, ratio, spacing, and arrangement of your

Corkboard. Using the buttons with square icons in the screenshot below, you can also toggle between snap-to-grid and freeform arrangements.

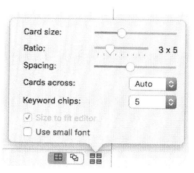

Another feature I like to use is auto-numbering for the index cards. To auto-number the cards, select "Show Card Numbers" in **View > Corkboard Options**. The screenshot below shows that option and a few others.

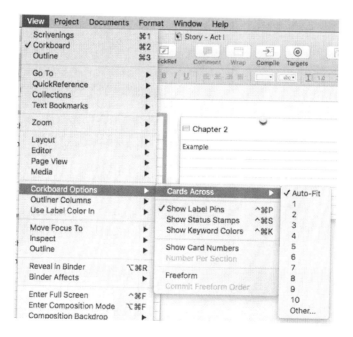

Finally, it's worth pointing out that the colors in the photo of my physical Corkboard came through because of the labels I applied to my scenes. I created labels for each point-of-view character (blue for the male lead, green for the female lead). You can turn on label colors by going to **View > Use Label Color In** and selecting where you want the colors to show. This comes through when you print them out, which has a nice visual effect. I'll go into more detail about labels in the chapter on Metadata.

Four Storyboarding Questions

Now that you can see your story as a whole in a physical medium, rearrange it and move cards around. Don't be afraid to mess it up, because your work is already saved in Scrivener at the point you printed it out. I find that seeing my story in a physical medium will reveal flaws I missed or couldn't see on a smaller computer screen.

Here are a few questions to ask yourself at this phase:

1. **Does each scene have a purpose?** If you remove a scene from your storyboard, what happens to your story? Make sure each scene contributes to the story in a meaningful way by revealing a new piece of information, developing your characters, and/or bringing your protagonist closer to (or farther from) their goal.

2. **Does your plot have continually rising action?**[13] Your story should have continually rising action so that the plot never goes slack or bores the reader. Read more about rising action online.

3. **Is there a consistent timeline?** Make sure that your timelines all match up, especially if you have multiple point-of-view characters. If your timeline is complex or difficult to keep track of, consider mapping it out in another tool called Aeon Timeline.[14] They also supply

specific documentation for integrating Aeon Timeline with Scrivener.[15]

4. **Have you hit all the important plot points?** You need an inciting incident, several scenes with rising action, a first plot point/doorway of no return, a second plot point/doorway of no return, a climax, and a resolution (at a minimum). Refer to the story craft books listed in the further reading recommendations if these terms for key story moments aren't familiar to you.

If you look closely at the photograph of my corkboard for *The Auriga Project*, you'll notice a couple edits that I made at this phase in the process. Can you spot them?

I added three scenes (and removed a few others.) Don't take this step for granted!

Then Make Changes in Scrivener

Once you've rearranged your story physically and you are happy with it, copy any changes you made back into Scrivener. I know this part is tedious, but keep in mind that all this work will make your story stronger—and make it easier for you to write it (or rewrite it!) when you are done.

Now, Start Writing Your Draft!

Finally, you're ready to start drafting. If you used this storyboarding process to outline a story you haven't yet written, here's what you do: duplicate your storyboard and drag the copy into the Manuscript folder of the Binder. If you haven't already done so, arrange the scenes into chapter folders.

Since you worked so hard to break the story out into scenes, your Manuscript is already arranged according to the best practices for structure in Scrivener that we covered earlier. You can then simply open the first scene and start typing. The description you wrote on the front of the index cards appears in the Synopsis section (top of the Notes pane in the Inspector), which makes it easy to reference while you're drafting.

The reason I suggest moving a copy of the storyboard you made instead of dragging the original over is that your story is going to continue to evolve as you write it. It's educational to compare the story you actually write to the storyboard you prepared once your draft is complete.

If, however, you used storyboarding to help you get unstuck or to revise your story at the end of a draft, you'll have to update your Manuscript folder to match your new outline. That means deleting scenes, moving scenes around, rearranging chapters, etc. Again, keep a copy of your storyboard for comparison later.

How to Start and Finish a Draft

You're Ready to Start Drafting

At this point, you've been introduced to the important pieces of Scrivener's user interface; you know how to structure your book; you know how to create character and setting sketches using Template Sheets; and you have a complete account of my storyboarding process for planning and getting unstuck while you're writing.

In other words, you have all the tools you need to start drafting.

Editor Settings

The blank page in the middle of Scrivener where you write your story, also called the Editor, is highly customizable. Before you begin, take a second to adjust your Editor settings. You'll be spending a lot of time here, so make sure everything is just how you like it.

You can manage the Editor Preferences by going to **Scrivener > Preferences** and adjusting the options in the Editor and Formatting panes.

SCRIVENER SUPERPOWERS

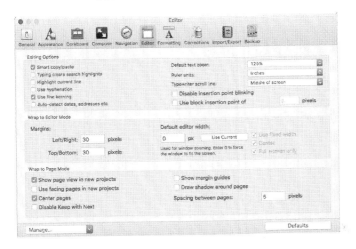

If you like to have a Ruler and Format Bar visible, you can hide/show those in the Menu under **Format > Show/Hide Ruler** and **Format > Show/Hide Format Bar**. I always have these showing so that I can adjust margins, alignment, and spacing quickly.

I also like to use Page View for fiction. You can turn Page View on in the Menu by going to **View > Page View > Show/Hide Page View**. If you're placing large images inline in your editor while you write (like I am with this book), you might want to turn Page View off so that you don't have blank spaces in your document when big images get bumped down to the next page.

Use settings that please you during the writing phase, because a happy writer is a productive writer. But also be aware that when you get to the compile phase, *you'll specify different formatting settings with Compile*. In other words, there is one group of settings that affects your Editor, and another group of settings that affects the formatting of the final document you generate with Compile. So if you want to write with blue Comic Sans text on a camouflage background, more power to you. That does not mean that those Editor formatting choices will carry over to your ebook or print book. We'll go over Compile in depth in a later chapter.

Full Screen Composition Mode

Did you know that Scrivener also has a distraction-free full screen Composition Mode? There should be a button in your Toolbar labeled Compose (a square icon with white arrows pointing at opposite corners of the square), or you can go to the Menu to find it: **View > Enter Composition Mode** or use the hotkey **Command+Option+f**.

Full screen Composition Mode is a great way to write when you want to eliminate distractions and focus on your work.

To change the settings of the Composition Mode, go to the Compose pane in your Preferences (**Scrivener > Preferences > Compose**):

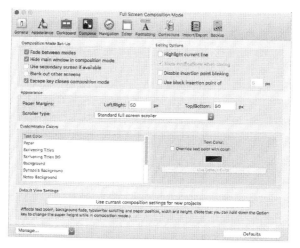

Just like the Editor, Compose is fully customizable. None of these settings will be reflected in your ebook when you compile, so adjust it to your heart's content.

In Compose, you can still access your Inspector panes and make other adjustments using the toolbar at the bottom of the screen. If it's not visible, hover your mouse at the bottom of the screen until it pops up. You may also change the background of

Composition Mode. I suggest uploading a photo of something relaxing, like a beach or forest or other natural landscape. To upload a new background photo go to **View > Composition Backdrop > Choose...** and pick a photo from your computer. Then adjust the Background Fade toggle in the Composition Mode toolbar (bottom right of your screen) so that the photo isn't distracting.

To exit Composition Mode, click the double arrows on the right of the Composition toolbar, or press Escape on your keyboard.

Notes, Comments, and Annotations

While you're writing, use the Document Notes, Comments, and Inline Annotations features to mark issues to fix later. This allows you to get a thought down without interrupting the creative flow state you enter while drafting. Don't resolve any of these comments, notes or annotations now. You'll come back to them during your first revision, *after* the draft is complete.

Here are the three types of comments/notes in Scrivener and how to use them.

Document Notes

There is a unique Document Notes section available for each text file and folder in the Binder. You can find it at the bottom of the Notes pane of the Inspector.

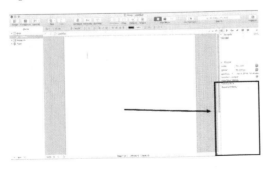

There's no right or wrong way to use this piece of the interface. When I first started using Scrivener, I had no idea what I would put there. Now, I fill it with all sorts of information about the scene I'm writing: How I feel about the scene, what's missing, a different way to approach the scene, what I like about it, a reminder to look up a piece of technology or do research on a topic, an idea for another scene, and even ideas for new stories.

Comments

The benefit of using this feature, as opposed to making a note in the Document Notes section, is that clicking on the comment takes you to the comment's place in your text, so it's easy to use comments to jump around your manuscript.

Inline Annotations

The third commenting feature is called Inline Annotations. Adding an Inline Annotation turns the annotated text red and draws a red box around it. This makes the annotation stick out like a sore thumb, and I use them for anything I don't know yet—for instance, characters or places that need a name (or need to be re-named). I might also use Inline Annotations on any phrasing that is questionable but which I don't have time or brainpower to work through at the moment.

> Character name was playing basketball with his friends.
>
> When all of a sudden…
>
> Boom! A meteorite struck the apartment building down the street.

Say you want to use the name of a city your characters have traveled to, but you haven't named the city yet—perhaps you just invented it. To prevent interrupting your flow, hit the shortcut **Command+Shift+A** for Inline Annotation, type "Name of city" (it will appear in red in your Editor like the screenshot above), and simply move on. The annotation will remind you that you need to fix it later when you come across it during the revision phase. That way, you're marking the issue to be fixed without interrupting your flow.

Storyboard If You Get Stuck

If you come up against a block or a particularly sticky plot issue that you can't plow through, take a step back and return to your storyboard. Ask yourself why you stopped writing and brainstorm ways to fix the problem.

When I get stuck during drafting, I'll first pick up my notebook and a pen and start journaling about the problem I've run into to find the core issue that caused my dilemma. Whether you like to write by hand when you do this or you prefer to type, I recommend doing this *outside* of Scrivener because the change of surroundings (and medium) will spark connections in your brain and give you a break from pounding your head against the same wall.

Once you identify what the problem is, revise your storyboard until you've found an effective fix.

When you are happy with your storyboard again or you have pinpointed the issue, make those changes in Scrivener and carry on writing.

Start Writing!

All right, no more procrastination. You've done the necessary planning. All that's left is to put words on the page.

Get a cup of coffee or tea. Take a deep breath—or three.

Now put your butt in that chair and start typing.

How to Set Targets and Measure Your Progress

As much as writing is an art, it is also a craft. It involves learned skills. And like a carpenter who can measure the dimensions of his materials, so too can writers measure the output of their work.

In other words, the craft of writing is *quantifiable*.

Every story is made up of words that you can count. *War and Peace* is roughly 250,000 words. *Of Mice and Men* is about 30,000 words. Fiction magazines typically accept short stories to a maximum of 7,000 words, depending on the publication. And their payment rates are often advertised per word.

In college, my professors used to assign essays based on the number of pages required. Write a ten-page essay on Shakespeare's *Hamlet*, for instance. This led to a lot of font-size and margin-adjustment cheating, thereby inadvertently putting focus on the wrong goal.

I wish they had given me word counts instead. I wish they had told me that with an average of 250 words per double spaced page, a ten-page essay is roughly the equivalent of 2,500 words. It would have made more sense to me and prevented any gaming of the system through sizing changes. It would also have given me a better sense of my rate of production as a writer and made me ask important questions earlier, like: How much effort goes into a thousand words? And how much time do you need to spend to produce that result?

Years later, when I started researching how to submit short fiction, I realized that writing was quantifiable. I started to do the math and very quickly learned that if I just got the words out every day, eventually I'd be holding a story in my hands. If I wrote

1,000 words a day, after a week I'd have a short story; after sixty days, I'd have a novel. It's that simple, and simple is manageable.

To get a sense of how to quantify a story, here are some generally accepted standards for word counts in fiction:

- Microfiction/flash fiction: Up to 1,000 words
- Short story: 1,000 – 10,000 words
- Novelette: 10,000 – 30,000 words
- Novella: 30,000 – 50,000 words
- Novel: 50,000+ words

You can use these numbers and a good sense of your rate of production to schedule your work and measure your progress. (If you are wondering what lengths of work a certain market accepts, look at a tool like Duotrope[16] or The (Submission) Grinder[17] to research markets, find out what kind of work they accept, and learn what they pay for each accepted submission.)

So that begs the question: How do you figure out what your rate of production is?

Learn by Experimentation

Are you familiar with the scientific method? Here's a simplified version: Step one, come up with a good question. Step two, run an experiment to test your hypothesis. Step three, compare your hypothesis to the results of your experiment. Step four, create a new hypothesis based on your newly acquired knowledge, and try it again.

Writers can follow the same process. Since you work with words, your hypothesis should be pretty straightforward, but let me start you off with some basic questions to answer.

- How long does it take me to write 1,000 words?
- Am I most productive in the mornings, afternoons, evenings, or nights?
- What is a sustainable daily word count goal for me?

- How can I change my schedule to make time for writing every day?

It's really important for my own process that I keep track of my daily word count. This gives me the feeling of motion and a sense of making progress. Most importantly, keeping track of my progress teaches me more about myself and how I write.

For example, after writing the first draft of my first novel (and keeping track in my notebook of how many words I wrote each day), I learned that my average word count is around 1,000 words per day. Pretty standard, right? What I didn't expect to learn was that I can get up to 2,500 words on a really great day, but that my bad days can be in the 300 word range—or less!

What a difference this kind of knowledge would have made in my essay writing days in college. Instead of cramming ten pages into the night before an assignment was due, I would have been encouraged to spread the work out over the amount of time it would take me to write it, and set achievable milestones. Once I discovered Scrivener, I did exactly that with my fiction.

You can do the same. Here's how you can use Scrivener to set targets and measure your progress.

Project Targets in Scrivener

Scrivener's Project Targets function (**Project > Show Project Targets**) shows you two progress bars: one for Manuscript Target and one for Session Target.

Let's start with the more immediate one.

Session Target

> **Project Targets - Creative Writing with...**
>
> **Manuscript Target**
>
> 19,882 of 17,500 words
>
> **Session Target**   Reset
>
> 170 of 1,000 words
>
> Options...   Edit

The Session Target calculates how many words you typed today. By default, only words written in the compile group are included in the daily count. Typically, that includes all files in the Manuscript folder. That means any notes, outline adjustments, character sketches, setting sketches, and words typed in files stored outside of your Manuscript folder are *not* included in the Session Target. You can adjust this by clicking the **Options...** button in the Project Targets pane and unchecking "Count documents included in compile only" and/or checking "Count text written anywhere in the project."

> **Draft Target**
> ☑ Count documents included in compile only
> ☐ Target applies to current compile group only
> ☐ Deadline: 4/12/2011
>
> **Session Target**
> Reset session count at midnight
> ☑ Count text written anywhere in the project
> ☐ Allow negatives
> ☐ Automatically calculate from draft deadline
> Writing days: ☐ Sun ☐ Mon ☐ Tue ☐ Wed ☐ Thu ☐ Fri ☐ Sat
>   ☐ Allow writing on day of deadline
> ☐ Show target notifications
>
>   OK

If you're in the planning phase, you may want to consider including your research material in the count so you can measure your research production rate. You can choose whether or not to include a document in the compile group by navigating to the Notes section of the Inspector for any particular file and checking the "Include in Compile" checkbox.

```
Label:           No Label
Status:          No Status
Modified:   ◇   Nov 24, 2015, 2:29 PM
Include in Compile                    ☑
Page Break Before                     ☐
Compile As-Is                         ☐
```

Scrivener also provides additional options for project targets, such as deadline and when to reset the session count. You'll find these in the **Options...** menu described above.

As I mentioned earlier, my personal session target goal is usually 1,000 words on a normal day. If you're unsure of your own production rate, a thousand words per day is a good place to start. But be sure to adjust your goal to fit your schedule and experience.

Manuscript Target

The other progress bar in the Project Targets screen is the Manuscript Target. Use this to set your word count target for the entire book you're currently writing.

Employ the word counts listed above for each type of fiction story to give you an idea of a general target for the type of work you're writing. If what you're writing isn't listed there, check out other books in your genre and estimate their word counts to give you a sense of the market.

My Manuscript Target is never perfect the first time. The goal is not to be exact, but to set a target to work toward. You can adjust your target as you write, so don't overthink it.

SCRIVENER SUPERPOWERS

Once you decide on a number for your Manuscript Target and Session Target, click the **Edit** button on the Project Targets screen, type the word count in the highlighted fields, and then click **Apply** to set it.

View Progress in the Outliner

Scrivener also makes word counts by folder and scene easily visible.

To get a holistic view of this, here's a screenshot of the Outliner of this book at an early phase in the drafting process.

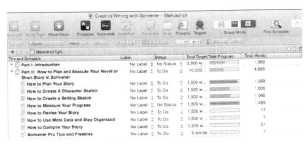

In order to see your work in the Outliner, click the third Group/View Mode button in the Toolbar. Currently I'm viewing the whole manuscript, but I could click into any folder if I wanted a narrower view.

The right-hand column showing Total Words is not visible by default. I added it because I like to see the word count of each section of my project. To add that column to your screen, click on the arrow to the right of the column headers and select Total Words from the list of column options that appear.

Finally, the Total Progress bar in the second-to-last column shows a visual measure of your recorded word count compared to the target you've set for that file/folder. You also have to add this column to your Outliner if you'd like to see it.

95

Setting Targets by Scene

Scrivener gives you the ability to set the word count targets not just for your manuscript or for your current writing session, but for each section of your book as well. However you break up your story, you can estimate length and plan your production by setting targets at the scene level.

To set the word count Target of a document, open and find the Target icon in the lower right-hand corner of the Editor. Here's a close-up:

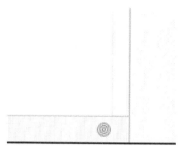

When you click on the icon, you'll be asked to set the Target for this document:

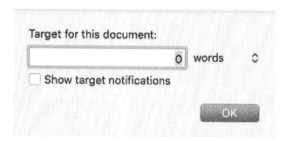

Another way to do this it to is to reveal the Target column in the Outliner view, and double click on the cell to edit the Target that way.

Now go through and set the word count Target on each document in your outline or storyboard. When that's done, you'll be able to estimate how long your complete manuscript will be. You can use this number to set your Manuscript Target if you haven't already done so.

One warning: Scrivener's Session Target count is calculated as the net total of your words. If you type 1,000 new words, then delete 300 words, your current day's session target will read 700 words.

The daily word count is just a tool to help you keep yourself accountable. What's important is how your progress tracks over time, so be kind to yourself.

Tracking Your Progress Over Time

Unfortunately, while Scrivener does a great job of tracking your progress in your current session, and while it does an even better job of making the word count visible across your entire manuscript, it does an absolutely terrible job of tracking word count over time, let alone tracking word count across multiple projects.

We're going to have to create our own progress tracking tool that we can use on a daily basis. There's no doubt in my mind that tracking progress over time is important. It's what all your daily inputs—of any size—eventually add up to that really matter. Here are a few different options for tracking your progress over time.

You can write your daily word count in a notebook or in a Project Note in Scrivener. To use a Project Note, go to **Project > Project Notes** in the Menu, create a new note named "Word Count," and record your progress there every day.

Be sure to include *at least* the date, what you were working on, and the number of words you got down. I used this method for several months on my first novel. After I finished the rough draft, I also wrote a blog about my word count goals and results[18] for that project. Check it out to see detailed graphs of my word count progress over time as well as lessons learned.

My preferred method to store word count data, however, is a spreadsheet. I store my spreadsheet in Google Drive.

The columns across the top are labeled:

- Date
- Project name
- Word count
- Time started
- Time ended
- Notes (How I felt, any problems I encountered and anything else that comes to mind)

Every day, I record what I've done in the spreadsheet and check to see how I'm tracking against my goals.

I give you these options to show you what's possible. You have to create a system and a process that works for you. Tracking words and optimizing your production is vital to the writing life. When you traffic in words, when your ability to pay the rent and put food on the table depends on your writing, why would you not want to keep track of your rate of production?

When Are You Most Productive?

In *2k to 10k* Rachel Aaron also suggests keeping track of the *hours* in which you write, so that you can calculate a words per hour figure. This is smart, and it's the reason I include "Start Time" and "End Time" columns in my spreadsheets.

Her reasoning is that by keeping this data, she found out what time of day was the most productive time for her (i.e. what time of day yielded the most words per hour on average). That's valuable. If you don't know when you are most creative and productive, find out.

I already know that I am most creative and productive in the morning. My mind is sharpest and the world is the quietest in the early hours. Those are my most productive hours, but yours might be in the afternoon, evening, or late at night. Only you will be able to tell when you're most productive, and the way you come to this conclusion is by thorough experimentation with diligently recorded results.

If your schedule is less flexible or you have to write in the margins of the day—before work, at lunch, on the train ride to work—I'd say forget this advice and write as much as you can during your writing sessions. Be sure to keep those sessions sacred and focused. Make use of the time you have.

After all, writing is simple. When you boil it down, all it takes is effort over time. That's powerful knowledge, and that knowledge will help you finish your manuscript.

How to Use Metadata and Stay Organized

Once you get into your draft, your workspace may get a little chaotic.

Embrace it. Make a mess. That's part of the creative process, and one of the benefits of using Scrivener is that you can wrangle that mess back into order at the end of your draft with relative ease. As long as you broke your story down into scenes in the planning phase like we discussed, you can drag and drop to rearrange later, and jump quickly through your story to make revisions and edits.

If you're like me, though, you'll want to have a system in place that allows for chaos without letting your story get out of control or—worse—overwhelming you. Scrivener gives you many ways to stay organized through a messy writing process.

They call it Meta-Data (though the common spelling is "metadata"). If you're not familiar with the term, metadata is a set of data that describes and gives information about other data. In the case of your book, that means data on your scenes, chapters, and other documents and folders within your book. Word count of a scene is a piece of metadata. Other metadata includes point of view (Old Man Ford, Bad Guy the Villain), setting (Old Man Ford's House, Police Station), status (To Do, First Draft, Revised Draft, Final Draft), or anything else you can come up with.

Here are several ways to stay organized with Scrivener Meta-Data and how it can make your life easier during the writing process.

Meta-Data Settings

To access the Meta-Data Settings, go to **Project > Meta-Data Settings...** in the Menu.

This is a screenshot of the Project Properties pane. You can change your book title and your author name here. These values will be used later when you compile your story for editing or publication.

Labels and Color Coding

The next pane is Labels. You can change the title "Labels" at the top of this pane and add as many values as you like. I like to use this one for "Point of View" and name the values after my characters. The screenshot, however, shows Scrivener's defaults.

I also color-code the labels I use. This is part of the reason I like using POV as the Label, because then I can easily see in the Outliner view how many of my scenes are from each character's POV simply by their color-coded arrangement. It allows me to check at a glance where one character might be hogging the spotlight, or where another character's POV is missing from an important part of the book. Here's what my novel *The Auriga Project* looks like in the Binder with POV color-coding:

```
▼ 📁 Manuscript
  ▼ 📁 The Demonstration
       📄 Chapter 1: The Demonstration
       📄 Chapter 1: Flashback
       📄 Chapter 1: Gift
  ▶ 📁 The Auriga Project
  ▶ 📁 Two Moons and a Purple Sky
  ▶ 📁 Scouring the Stars
  ▶ 📁 Healer, Shaman, Chief
  ▶ 📁 Unknown Agents
  ▶ 📁 The Color of Sacrifice
  ▶ 📁 Lockdown
  ▶ 📁 Life in Kakui
  ▶ 📁 Threats and Intimidation
  ▶ 📁 Uchben Na
  ▶ 📁 Breaking and Entering
  ▶ 📁 The Legend of Ky and Kai
  ▶ 📁 The Blast Door
  ▶ 📁 Survival Kit
  ▶ 📁 Leap of Faith
  ▶ 📁 Second Sacrifice
  ▶ 📁 The Well of Sacrifices
  ▶ 📁 Breaking News
  ▶ 📁 Beyond the Wall
```

You have to turn the color-coding on if you want it to be visible in the Outliner or Binder. In the Menu go to **View > Use Label Color** In to customize it to your liking. I like the Icons option (pictured above).

Status

Status can be used however you like. Add statuses until they match your writing process. Scrivener comes with decent defaults, but don't be afraid to customize it. Need four drafts before the final? Want to have a "Waiting on Editorial Feedback" or "Beta read" status? Great! Add them.

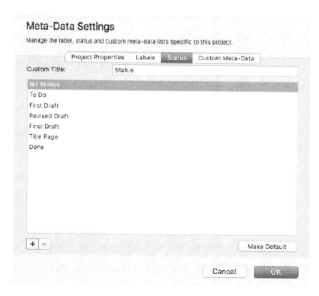

Both Labels and Statuses are also editable on each scene in the General section of the Inspector (visible in Notes, References, and Keywords panes). Just open the dropdown you want to change, click **Edit...** at the bottom, and it will take you to the Meta-Data Settings pane to edit them.

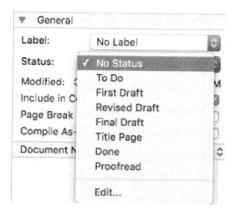

Custom Meta-Data

Custom Meta-Data is the last pane in Meta-Data Settings, and a very powerful one for further customization. You might want to add setting, motivation, or anything else to your outline to stay organized. Make the custom metadata you add visible in the Outliner by right clicking on the column headers of the Outliner and selecting your Custom Meta-Data field to be visible as a column.

It's worth mentioning that I don't use these too much. If you can't find a use for Custom Meta-Data, either, it can be safely ignored.

Custom Icons

The Binder also supports custom icons. Right click on an icon next to any file/folder in the Binder to select a new icon.

I like to use the icons to differentiate large sections of my project, like Manuscript, Research, Cut Scenes, Sales Copy, and Outline.

There are plenty of icons to keep you happy, but if you want to add your own custom icons you can do so by going to **Documents > Change Icon > Manage Icons...** from the Menu. You'll need to use a supported icon image format, so don't do try this unless you're familiar with digital imaging formats and software like Photoshop or Illustrator.

I find that the icons that come with Scrivener provide plenty of options to suit my daily writing needs.

Folders and Subfolders

    Finally, keep in mind that the Binder is extremely flexible, and you can add as much (or as little) as you want to it. In this document I currently have the following containers: Manuscript, Proposal, Marketing, Competition, Outline/Chapter Synopsis, Notes, Ideas, and Research. And that's not even counting all the files.

    Don't let yourself get overwhelmed. Collapse folders for easy viewing, create organizational systems to make your life easier (and your mind clearer), and drag and drop to move files and folders around.

How to Revise Your Story

Once your first draft is complete, your next order of business is to revise it.

Most authors go through several drafts. I typically write at least four drafts of a story, and I read it dozens of times. Everyone is different, but for the beginners out there, a warning: don't make the mistake of thinking your first draft is anywhere near good enough for publication. Writers are terrible judges of their own work, myself included.

Fortunately, Scrivener's Snapshot function and other revision features take a lot of the fear out of revising by giving you a way to capture your draft. You can then add comments, make revisions, and easily revert back if the changes you made don't work like you hoped.

Rest Your Manuscript

First of all, you finished a draft: Congratulations! It's time to celebrate.

You've still got a lot of work to do, but it's important to celebrate the small victories. Go out with your friends. Open a nice bottle of wine. Treat yourself to a massage to work out the cramped neck muscles you acquired from bending over your laptop and typing furiously as you flew toward the end of your story.

Before you dig into your revisions, I suggest taking at least a week to rest your manuscript. Possibly longer, but no more than a couple months. How long you can afford to rest it is entirely dependent on your own process and level of comfort, but don't sit idle in the meantime. Write a couple short stories or start another book to keep your craft muscles fit and your mind engaged.

Taking space and time off is the only way to see your manuscript with fresh eyes without enlisting the help of others. While you're away, your subconscious mind will work on it without the necessity for active thought. New ideas will occur to you in the oddest places—in the shower, at the gym, in bed before you fall asleep. Subconscious thinking is one wonderful aspect of the human brain.

When you're ready, sit down and open your story with a positive outlook.

Now, the real work begins.

Take Snapshots

Whether you just finished draft one or you are about to start draft four, kick off each revision with a Snapshot of every scene. Unfortunately, you can't take a Snapshot of an entire Scrivener project in a single click. You'll have to go through scene by scene and take individual Snapshots. It will only take a few minutes and will be well worth the effort.

To take Snapshots, start at your first scene, and open the Snapshots pane of your Inspector. (The button to open it looks like a little camera.) Click the plus (+) at the top (or in the Menu select **Documents > Snapshots > Take Snapshot**). Then name your Snapshot after your draft version. If this is the first Snapshot, call it something like "Draft 1." You'll thank yourself for naming them in later drafts, when you have multiple Snapshots of each scene.

With every scene captured, you now have an undo button for your story; you can safely revise without fear of losing work or screwing something up.

If you ever need to revert back to your Snapshot, simply navigate to the Snapshots pane, select the draft you want to revert back to, and click the **Roll Back** button. You can't undo a Roll Back, so make sure you take another Snapshot before going through with it, just in case you change your mind. Scrivener will remind you to take a Snapshot if you try to Roll Back.

Resolve Your Comments and Annotations

Is the fear of revising going away yet?

Next, you'll want to resolve all of those Document Notes, Comments, and Inline Annotations you added during the messy drafting phase.

Remember how you can click the Comments to jump to their location in the text? That's a handy feature here. Start with the easy ones you know how to resolve, thanks to the time you took to rest your manuscript and all the work your subconscious has done in the meantime. Click on the Comment to jump to it, and then fix whatever was bothering you during your draft.

Don't worry if it's not a perfect fix. Just resolve the inconsistency, error, or missing research. Then delete the comment and move on. If you find yourself agonizing over word choice or grammar, snap yourself out of it. There will be plenty of time for copyediting and proofreading later. Focus on filling in the gaps and getting your story onto the page.

Also resolve all of your Document Notes (if you took any) and Inline Annotations.

We'll go over advanced search techniques in the Scrivener Tips for Pros chapter, but since you're resolving Inline Annotations now, it's worth mentioning that you can find them easily using the search function. In the Menu, go to **Edit > Find > Find by Formatting...** and select "Inline Annotations" from the dropdown. Neat, right?

Red Pen Read-Through

Now that all of the Comments and Annotations are resolved and any gaps you left during your first draft are filled, you're ready for the first full read-through.

I like to print out my story and do a full read-through on paper. Reading on paper is better for your eyes than reading on a screen, and seeing the story in a different medium reveals flaws I missed on the computer.

To print, you can simply open the Manuscript folder and go to **File > Print Current Document**, or you can Compile the Manuscript to Word or PDF and print it out that way (Compile instructions are located in the next chapter).

In any case, sit down with your story and a red pen and start reading. Mark all the issues you see, including word choice, grammar, character motivation, and stilted dialogue. Be ruthless. This is your chance to be critical of your own work.

And take your time. This is not a process that can be rushed.

Once your read-through is complete, import all the changes you made back into Scrivener. Make changes directly to the text, and add bigger issues that still need work as Comments.

(If you prefer not to print out the story, do your full read-through in Scrivener and instead of a red pen, simply add Comments. The end result will be the same; it's simply a matter of preference.)

At the end of this process, you will have made a lot of changes, and you'll have dozens of new comments to resolve. Don't forget to take a new Snapshot!

Drag and Drop to Restructure

You might already have started to make structural changes during your red pen read-through.

That's good. You will want to make those big structural changes first. There's nothing worse than fiddling for hours with sentences and paragraphs only to realize that the scene you were working on actually has no place in the story and needs to be cut.

A successful revision is a matter of getting the structure right *first*. Perhaps one of your POV characters doesn't have a complete arc and they need several new scenes. Maybe you wrote chapters in an order that doesn't support continually rising action or increased stakes, or you wrote past the climax of a scene, or a scene is in the wrong chapter, or ... you get the point.

Scrivener makes the structural edit easier than ever, and this is one of the great advantages of breaking your story down into scenes in the Binder early in the planning phase. Instead of cutting and pasting big chunks of text like you might have done in a linear word processor, you can *drag and drop scenes within the Binder to rearrange them*.

The first task I'll undertake after my red pen read-through is to restructure the story, if necessary. I make new text documents for missing scenes, rearrange the ones that are there so they're in the proper order, and validate my structure with what I know about story craft.

Revise Your Story Free of Fear

Now that you've fixed the structure of your story, you're ready to revise. Everyone has their own method for revising a story, so I'm not going to tell you what to do first other than to reiterate that you should make the large changes up front. Fix the big problems first, and save the small fiddly issues for later.

Delete comments and annotations as you resolve them. Snapshot again after you finish revising a scene. Take as many Snapshots as you need. Knowing your work is saved and version-controlled will allow you to revise free of fear.

Comparing Snapshots

You can revert back to a previous Snapshot if whatever change you made during the revision process didn't have the effect you intended. Before you do so, compare Snapshots to see what changed and why your changes didn't work, and learn from the experience. Perhaps the side-by-side comparison will help you see where you went astray.

To compare Snapshots, navigate to the Snapshots pane of your Inspector, select the Snapshot you want to compare to the current version, and click the **Compare** button.

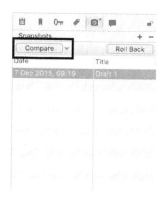

Version Entire Projects

For drafts where you are doing a lot of rewriting (as opposed to the less intensive *revising*), or where you suspect the end result might be a totally different story and not even Snapshots put your mind at ease, go ahead and duplicate the Scrivener project.

I name my projects with version numbers (1.0, 1.1, 2.0, 2.1, 2.2, etc.) when I duplicate a file. For example, my first novel started out as a short story (1.0), which I revised heavily (1.1). When I started expanding it into a novel, I duplicated the file (2.0) so that I could make huge changes and expansions without losing the work I had already done. Versioning my story went a long way toward setting my mind at ease.

I finished the book at version 2.3.

How to Compile Your Story

Once your story is revised and you're happy with the way the current draft turned out, it's time to share it with the world.

Whether you plan to submit it to an agent, send it to an editor, run it by your beta readers, or publish the book, you'll be using Compile to generate the files you need.

More than just printing or saving, Compile is the process by which you lay out your story and export it in the desired format. Using this robust feature you can generate files such as ebooks (.epub, .mobi), Word documents (.doc or .docx), Rich Text files (.rtf), PDFs (for printing and/or print book interior), and other file types.

Compile Is One of Scrivener's Most Powerful Features

Why is Compile so powerful?

Say you're one of those writers who likes to customize your Editor. The fonts and margins have to be *just right*. Or maybe you like a black background and green text—it makes you feel like you're in *The Matrix*.

If you wrote a short story and planned on submitting it to a magazine, this format would be unacceptable by their standards. Most magazines only accept stories for submission in Standard Manuscript Format—Courier font, 12 point, double spaced, with page number and last name in the top right corner. (If you aren't familiar with Standard Manuscript Format, you can find examples online.[19])

With Scrivener, you can customize your Editor to your heart's content *because Compile removes formatting from the equation.* You simply go to **File > Compile...**, select "Standard Manuscript Format," fill out any missing information, and *voila!* You have a manuscript in Standard Format, and you can still enjoy your crazy *Matrix*-style Editor.

Compiling for Submission and Publication

The second reason Compile is powerful is that it will save you a lot of effort in the digital publishing world.

If you're submitting short stories to magazines, for instance, you probably know that all magazines have different rules about what file types they accept for submission. If they take electronic submissions, sometimes they'll ask for a .docx, sometimes only a .doc. Sometimes they'll take a PDF; other times they'll require an RTF file. Sheesh! With so many options, how are you supposed to make everyone happy?

Compile will help. It allows you to simply and painlessly save your story in any format you could possibly need with relatively little effort.

If you're self-publishing, this is a game changer. No longer do you need to hire someone to format your ebooks and print-on-demand files for the various retailers. You can do it all with Scrivener, and upload the files you generate directly to distributors like Kindle Direct Publishing at Amazon, Kobo, Nook, iBooks, etc.

Compiling for an Editor or Proofreader

Whatever kind of work you're doing, you're likely working with an editor.

Independent authors submit directly to an editor. If you get picked up by a traditional publisher, you'll have to submit your manuscript to an agent first, and later to an editor at the publishing house.

However you get there, if you are working with an editor, they'll probably want your manuscript in a format that allows them to track changes.

In my experience, this means Microsoft Word. It's not ideal, but it's still the preferred tool for tracking changes.

Not that you can't have an editor leave comments and suggest changes directly in Scrivener using a combination of Comments and Snapshots. You certainly *can* do that, if your editor is willing. This book has already taught you how—just use the same process we discussed in the chapter on revision, but do it with two people.

However, Microsoft Word's change tracking features are simply more robust when it comes to editing. They give you a way to accept/reject changes, to see the edits, and to allow multiple people to track changes in the same document.

After your editor makes their changes and leaves comments in your Word document, you'll want to bring the comments and changes *back* into Scrivener for your next revision. I go through the manuscript one page at a time and carry the changes over to Scrivener manually. Two reasons: one, I want to learn from my editor's work; two, I like to stay organized.

You may also copy and paste the text back into Scrivener (after you take a Snapshot, of course). Any comments remaining in the Word document will be carried into Scrivener. The suggested changes, however, will not make it over, so use this approach with caution.

Compiling for Beta Readers

You might also want to export your story for your beta readers. It's important to give beta readers the best experience possible, which is why I Compile my story in various formats and send it to them in the format they prefer. For instance, say that one likes to use Word, another prints it out, and a third likes to read on their iPad. I might send a .docx to the first person, a PDF to the second, and an .epub or .mobi file to the third.

You want your readers to be happy. Give them what they want. In turn, they'll read your story and give you the feedback you ask for.

Compile is a Rules-Based Generator

By now you should have given some thought to what files you want to use Compile to generate. Now let's take a moment to talk about what Compile is.

The best way to think about Compile is as a rules-based generation system.

What does that mean? Basically, Compile takes your Scrivener project and generates your desired file based on the rules you provide to the Compiler. In that way, it's a lot like a programming compiler. If you've ever programmed before, you'll pick up Compile pretty quickly. If not, you may have to be a little more patient because it requires a mode of thinking you're probably not used to, especially if you learned to format books another way (like in Word).

There are benefits and drawbacks to the rules-based approach. On the one hand, it removes some of the elements of human error. For instance, your chapter titles and section breaks each have their own rules, so they will always be formatted consistently. On the other hand, it also means that you have to set up your book in a consistent way from the beginning.

Compile is *not* good for all books. Some books you'll have a lot of trouble formatting in Scrivener are children's books and books with lots of visuals and text wrapping.

For novels, short stories, and most nonfiction, Compile works like a charm.

Compile, Summary Tab

Now that you know whom you're compiling for and what file type you need, let's go into the Compile process in more detail.

Start by going to **File > Compile...** to bring up the Compile options screen. Then switch over to the Summary tab at the top so that we can start with the basics.

As you can see in the screenshot, I've selected the preset "Standard Manuscript Format" as my desired output. By default, this makes the "Compile For" dropdown at the bottom select "Print." If I clicked Compile now, it would open the print screen on my computer, where I could print the book or save it to my computer.

You may change the file type output using the "Compile For" dropdown to generate another type of file, such as a Word Doc, RTF, PDF, or ebook. Since we're using the Standard Manuscript Format preset, the formatting will be done automatically.

The other features to take note of on the summary screen are:

- **Compile dropdown.** This is where you choose the folders/documents to include in the generated file. In the above screenshot, I've got the Manuscript folder selected. That's usually what you'll want there.

- **Front Matter dropdown.** This is where you choose which folder or file you're using for your front matter. For Standard Manuscript Format, this means simply a title page, as I have selected above. What you select here depends on what you want to be displayed at the front of your book.

- **Formatting checkboxes.** Do what you like with these. I don't really like when they convert my italics to underlines, but the option is there for you.

- **Font dropdown.** You can choose what font you want the generated file to use. Right now I've got "Determined by Document Style" selected, which means whatever font I was using in my Editor, but you can choose whatever font you prefer. Keep in mind that if you're generating an ebook file (.mobi or .epub), ereading devices override the font of the document based on the user's settings, so this option will not be present.

If I change the "Format As" preset to generate an ebook, the Summary tab changes:

Now I get a different set of options. The "Compile" and "Front Matter" dropdowns are still there (notice how the "Font" dropdown is missing), but instead of the formatting checkboxes you are asked to enter:

- **Title**. This is the title of your book that is shown on the ereader. It is automatically filled with the metadata you provided in the Meta-Data Settings we talked about in How to Use Metadata and Stay Organized. You can type a new title to override these settings.

- **Authors**. This is where you type your author name(s). This field is also automatically filled out based on your Meta-Data Settings, but you can type something else to override it.

- **Cover image**. This is where you choose your cover image. You can only choose an image that exists in your Scrivener file, so make sure you drag your cover into your Scrivener file first (I keep my cover image in my Front Matter folder).

- **Generate HTML table of contents**. This is a handy option. Scrivener can generate a table of contents at the front of the ebook for you.

- **Remove comments and annotations**. Always check this box unless you want your editorial comments and annotations to show up in the ebook for some reason.

- **Compile For**. Note how the "Compile For" option was changed to "ePub eBook (.epub)" when I switched the preset to compile an ebook. If you're looking to generate a .mobi ebook for Amazon, simply change this dropdown to "Kindle eBook (.mobi)."

Other Compile Presets

So far on the Summary pane of Compile we've used two presets: Standard Manuscript Format and E-Book.

Scrivener provides several other Compile presets. If you open the "Format As" dropdown and then click "Manage Compile Format Presets..." you can see them all.

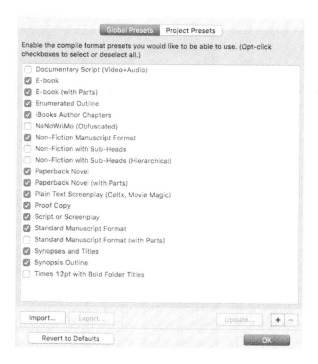

These presets provide the formats that most people need. You can also import presets and export them. If you find yourself using the same custom Compile options for all of your books, you might want to consider creating a preset to save yourself repeated effort.

For beginners, I recommend using presets. They do a lot of the hard work for you and are a good place to start learning how Compile works. Save your book in the format of your choice, open it to see how it looks, and make adjustments from there.

All Options Tab

Once you've mastered the Summary tab and are ready to customize your formatting and generated files to your liking, head over to the All Options tab.

You can still use presets in the "All Options" tab. As you can see, I've chosen to stick to the preset "E-book" and generate a "Kindle eBook (.mobi)" file. (Note: for Kindle books, you'll need to install KindleGen.)

Each file type you choose to generate exposes a different set of Compilation Options (the column on the left). Kindle eBook files have more Compilation Options than most.

For comparison, check out the differences in the list when you choose to generate a Plain Text file:

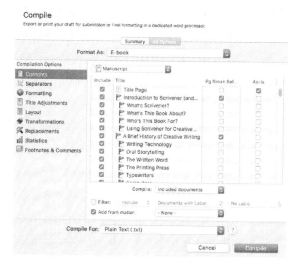

Once you start making significant changes, don't be surprised if the "Format As" dropdown changes to "Custom." It confused me the first time it happened (because I was fiddling with the settings so much), but it's totally normal. Once you begin to actually customize the Compiler for the options you need, you're no longer using a built-in preset, but your own "Custom" settings.

Contents Pane

Let's take another look at the Contents pane on the All Options tab and talk about the extra options available to you now.

SCRIVENER SUPERPOWERS

Just like on the Summary tab, you select what documents you want to include in the generated file by using a dropdown menu. As before, I've selected the Manuscript folder.

The Front Matter selector is at the bottom this time. Select your Front Matter folder or your title page, as you need.

The list in the middle is where the interface gets a little more confusing. From the left, let's go through the columns:

- **Include checkbox**. This is asking whether or not you want to include this document in the generated file. You can include/exclude files with finer control here. This is a very useful feature, especially when you're generating ebooks with slightly different Front Matter for different retailers.

- **Title**. The title of the document in question. Nothing to change here.

- **Page Break Before**. This checkbox is asking whether

you want the generated file to include a page break before the beginning of the item in question. Notice how I've chosen to include a page break before the beginning of each chapter. That's standard practice in book formatting. You want some white space to give the reader a breather between chapters, and a chance to reflect on what they've just read.

- **As-Is**. Compile will ignore the formatting settings of your Editor unless you check the "As-Is" box. If you check this box, the *exact* formatting you put in your Editor will be carried over to the Compiled file. I use this option for title pages, copyright pages, table of contents pages, or any other pages where the formatting needs to be precise and blank space must be preserved. Copyright pages, for instance, often have blank space at the top of them. This option is also very useful when generating print books, whose formatting is more exact than ebooks.

Separators Pane

The next Compilation Options pane is called Separators.

In this section you can specify what you want to insert between sections. You can specify the separator for text documents, folders, folders and text, and text and folders.

There's a description below each one so that you don't get confused. For instance, a text separator "will be inserted between adjacent text documents."

In novels, this is the marker denoting scene breaks. Some authors like to use an empty line (and I've got "Empty line" selected above). Others prefer three asterisks, or three dots, or a pound sign. Type the separator you want to use into the field.

These fields will take return carriages (i.e. new lines) as well as special characters.

Cover Pane

The next Compilation Options pane for ebooks is Cover. You simply choose your cover image here.

As a reminder, you won't have the Cover option if you're generating a file without a cover, like a Word Doc or a Plain Text file.

Formatting Pane

The next pane is Formatting. This one is where a lot of your customization will occur, and it's where an understanding of the rules-based generation system makes a big difference.

Section Type List

In the list taking up the top half of the Formatting pane, you'll see three rows with icons: a folder, a group of documents, and a single document. They all say "Level 1+" next to them, which denotes their document's level of nesting within the binder.

In order to see how the hierarchy applies to your files, click on a row; the corresponding folders/files to which the rules of this item apply will be highlighted in the Binder (the highlighting only occurs on the Mac, but the same hierarchy concept applies for both Mac and Windows). See below how when I select the "Level 1+" folder, all of the folders in my Binder are highlighted (I have flag icons on the folders in the screenshot; don't worry about those, they have nothing to do with Compile, they just help me keep track of edits).

If you select the single text document, all of the files visible within the folders would be highlighted in the Binder (the opposite of what is highlighted in the screenshot).

What this means is that any rules you apply to that list item will be applied, in the generation of the file, to all of the highlighted Binder items associated with that item.

You can add and remove levels of hierarchy for complex manuscripts using the +/- buttons at the top right of the pane.

Section Type List Options

The checkboxes to the right of each list item (Title, Meta-Data, Synopsis, Notes, and Text) allow you to choose what gets added for each file/folder during Compile. In the screenshot above, each chapter and group of files will show only the title, while each single file will show only the text of that file.

For this book, I'm relying on the names of the files to show the subheadings within my chapters. When I Compile, I make sure that the Title and Text checkboxes are ticked for all single documents and groups of documents. That way Compile will automatically generate my chapter titles and sub-headers consistently and with a minimal amount of effort.

Section Formatting

The bottom half of the Formatting pane allows you to customize the text and font styles for each item in the top half of the list. For instance, here's what it looks like when you choose to show only the text of a document with no title.

The Formatting pane has most of your normal text formatting options, such as alignment, bold/italic/underline, color and highlight, line spacing, font, and size.

The Options Button

There are more concealed options worth pointing out. The first set is hidden in an Options button at the top right of the Formatting pane. The other is behind a Section Layout button in the middle left area. You can see them both indicated in the screenshot on the right.

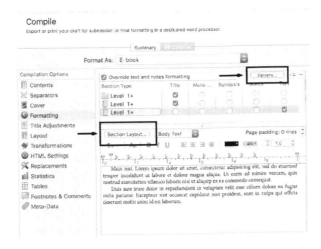

What's behind button number one in the Formatting pane, Options?

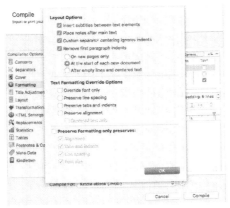

These checkboxes allow you to preserve alignment (or only preserve centered text, which I find really handy), remove first paragraph indents, and much more across the entire book.

Section Layout Button

The other set of options is hidden behind the Section Layout button. Where the previous Options button is for the entire book, the Section Layout options are unique to each Section Type list item.

It looks like this:

In these options you can:

- **Set Prefixes and Suffixes.** Prefixes are frequently used for auto-numbering chapters, like you see above. The word "Chapter" is typed in, and then the variable < $t > is used to generate the number of a chapter spelled out, i.e. one, two, three, etc. Note that the prefix and suffix will be displayed even if the title is disabled for this section, which can prove useful in some cases but inconvenient if you don't know about that rule. You can find a full list of variables in Scrivener by going to **Help > Placeholder Tags List.**...

- **Change Title Appearance.** In the middle tab of the Section Layout Options, you can, for instance, capitalize your titles.

- **First Page Appearance.** In the last tab, you can capitalize the first few words on a page, or indicate whether or not to always start a section on a recto (right) or verso (left) page.

The Formatting pane is very complex. If you need additional assistance, I highly recommend reading the dense but informative Scrivener Help Manual about this section.

Title Adjustments Pane

The Title Adjustments pane gives you several options for your titles. These are pretty self-explanatory, but here's a screenshot.

Layout Pane

Next is the Layout pane.

Here you'll find customizations for your automatically generated HTML table of contents, and a few other options.

Transformations Pane

Next is the Transformations pane, where you'll find several useful options for file-wide overrides.

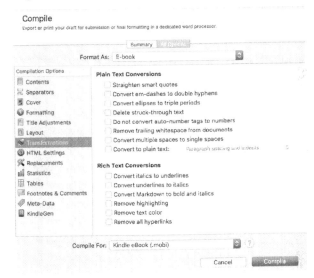

Page Settings Pane

The Page Settings pane is specifically for PDFs.

Scrivener can generate PDF files for print book interiors, which you can upload to print-on-demand services like CreateSpace and Lightning Source to create a print version of your book.

On this pane, you specify your margins (dependent on print size), your page header and footer, header/footer font choices, and more.

You can also use the Facing Pages tab to define alternate headings for your print book. For instance on the recto (right) page you can put your author name and page number at the top, and on the verso (left) page you can put the title and page number at the top.

While you'll need to go to a more robust design program like InDesign for complex print layouts, these Page Settings will allow you to format simple novels, short stories, and nonfiction manuscripts. I used it for my first novel with great success, and it kept me from having to spend money on a formatter to get what I wanted.

KindleGen

Lastly, to generate .mobi files for Kindle Direct Publishing at Amazon, you need to install the KindleGen script.

Once you select a Kindle eBook from the **"Compile For"** dropdown, a KindleGen pane will appear that looks similar to the screenshot above. Navigate to that pane, click the link to Amazon, and follow the instructions. You'll have to install the KindleGen script on your computer and show Scrivener where it is before you can generate a .mobi file.

Book Formatting Services

If Compile intimidates you, stick to the summary screen and the presets and you'll get a working file with a minimal amount of effort. Your ebook might not be perfect, but you can rest assured that it will get the job done.

If formatting simply isn't something you want to do, or you have a more complex book with nuanced formatting needs, locate a professional book formatter. Ask your writer friends for recommendations or contact authors who have well-formatted books and ask them for a referral. It's typically a very affordable service.

Test and Check

To have a good experience with Compile, you'll need to be okay with testing and checking your work. This requires patience and a willingness to do online research when you run into trouble.

In order to check the formatting of an ebook on your computer, start with ePub files and use iBooks to check your work. iBooks comes with every new Mac.

To preview Kindle files, download the Kindle Previewer[20] created by Amazon for independent publishers to check their Kindle files.

I'm also a fan of the Kindle reading apps for testing (and for reading after several drafts have been completed). Kindle apps[21] are available to download on all your computers and devices.

Lastly, the easiest way to get your Kindle files onto your devices for testing or reading is by using the Send To Kindle Email.[22]

Good luck!

Scrivener Tips for Pros

Next, I will show you several methods for importing content, a detailing of Scrivener's search functionality, and how to configure automated backups.

These advanced tips aren't required for the start-to-finish writing process we've covered in the previous chapters, but if you spend a lot of time in Scrivener, they will help you work better and more efficiently.

Importing Content

If you've got a lot of material stored in formats other than Scrivener and wish to move the content over to Scrivener, you have a few options.

These methods are useful whether you're importing your own work or if you're using Scrivener to format a book written by someone else in another word processor.

Copy and Paste

Option number one: Go through your original document, whether that's a Microsoft Word file or something else, and copy and paste the text one section at a time into corresponding files in a new Scrivener project.

Or, you can dump the whole manuscript into a single text document, and split it up in Scrivener after you close the other program.

Copying and pasting can be tedious and time consuming.

But, having worked with files that were given to me in other file formats (to write, edit, or format for publication), I find that it's the most reliable method for transferring content into Scrivener.

Nothing is lost or missing or broken because I oversee the transfer myself.

Import

Your second option, a more automated method, is to use the Import function found in the Menu under **File > Import > Files...**

This is a suitable alternative if you can't stomach a copy and paste session, but it's far from perfect. Import's job is simply to get the content into Scrivener, relying on the user to sort out the organization later.

In my opinion, you're better off copying and pasting the content into Scrivener manually.

Import and Split

You third and final option is somewhere between a manual and an automated process. It's called Import and Split, and you can find it in the Menu under **File > Import > Import and Split...**

This function asks you to determine what the "Sections are separated by:" in the file selection menu, and then breaks those sections out into separate files during the import.

For instance, let's say you have a novel manuscript in Microsoft Word, and your novel is broken down into 20 chapters.

What you do is go through *the original document* and place a unique marker at the end of each chapter that tells the Import and Split function where to create a new file in the Scrivener project during import.

Say you use three pound signs as the unique marker. First, make sure ### is not present anywhere else in the manuscript except where you want the file breaks to occur. Then, after making sure ### is at the end of each chapter:

1. Click on the folder you want to import the content to
2. Select **Import and Split...** from the Menu
3. Type your marker, ###, in the "Sections are separated by:" input
4. Choose your file from the file selection menu
5. Press enter.

Scrivener will then automatically break your 20 chapters out into separate files based on where you inserted the unique split marker.

If it doesn't break how you'd expect, simply delete the files from your Scrivener project and try again.

More Work Now, Less Headache Later

I hope you don't find the task of importing content into Scrivener a chore. It causes a little extra work now, but less headache in the long run, like straightening that paper-strewn desk in your office before you start writing, or cleaning out the junk drawer in your kitchen that always seems to fill up so quickly.

In other words, it's worth the effort.

Advanced Search

Advanced Search is one of my favorite features in Scrivener. It has saved me many headaches in the revision stage by helping me locate troublesome words and phrases (e.g. "the fact that", "that said", "was" and other weak words and phrases), find particular pieces of research material, and change names across entire projects.

Find

You can access all of the search functions in the Menu under **Edit > Find**. There, you'll find the following options:

- Find...
- Find Next
- Find Previous
- Use Selection for Find
- Jump to Selection
- Project Replace...
- Project Search...
- Find Synopsis...
- Find by Formatting...
- Find Next by Formatting
- Find Previous by Formatting

I'm not going to cover the Find functions you are likely familiar with (Find..., Find Next, Find Previous), and which come standard with many software programs, except to say that the normal search and replace function can be located in the **Find...** menu.

Project Search

What's far more interesting and useful are Scrivener's project-wide search and replace functions.

Because Scrivener is a nonlinear word processing tool, the normal Find function is limited to searching and replacing *only the current document*.

When you want to do a project-wide search/replace, you'll want to use the Project Search or Project Replace functions instead.

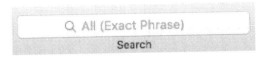

You can access the Project Search two ways: by locating **File > Project Search...** in the Menu, or by typing into the search field in the Toolbar.

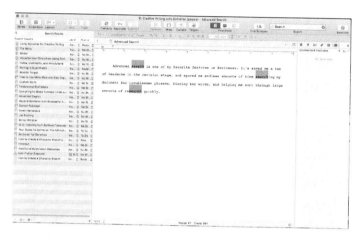

When you type into the search field, your Binder (the left-hand column in Scrivener) is replaced with your search results. It looks something like this:

The searched phrase is highlighted in the Editor, and you can use the Binder to jump between search results to quickly find what you're looking for.

To exit out of the search, click the gray X in the search bar.

Project Replace

Project Replace allows you to do a search and replace across an entire project.

Going to **File > Find > Project Replace...** in the Menu brings up this screen:

I've used the Project Replace with great success when:

- Changing names of characters across entire manuscripts
- Changing names of settings/locations
- Changing placeholder annotations or phrases to the final chosen phrase.

The extra options are fantastic for narrowing your search and replace by case, and to specific portions of text (e.g. you can uncheck Titles to exclude them from the search and replace).

Other Advanced Search Options

Finally, there are two more advanced search options worth mentioning.

Find Synopsis... only searches the Synopsis section of the Notes pane of the Inspector. In other words, the text you typed on the front of the index cards during your storyboarding process.

And **Find by Formatting...** allows you to search basically everything else: highlighted text, comments and footnotes, inline annotations, links, and more.

Automated Backups

Always, always, *always* back up your work.

In the past two days I've seen Facebook posts from two writers whose computers died. They lost large chunks of manuscripts they were working on.

They were both horrified and distraught. Don't let that happen to you!

To make your life easier and less stressful, Scrivener supports automatic backups. It's like magic! Simply navigate to the Backup pane of your Preferences, and configure what you find there:

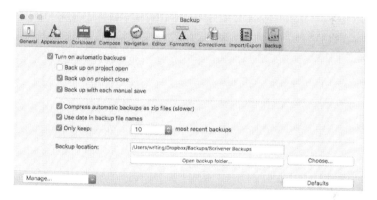

Super easy, right?

Don't forget to point the Backup location to a place where you'll remember how to find it later, if you need it. I'm a big fan of putting my Backup location in a folder in Dropbox for an added measure of security.

Let me explain: The desktop app of a cloud-storage service like Dropbox essentially puts a folder on your computer that is automagically synced to "the cloud." That means that there's a copy of those files on your computer, and another copy in "the cloud," which is a fancy way of saying, "file servers on the other side of the world."

If you don't know what the cloud is, don't worry too much. What's important is that when your files are in the cloud, even if your computer breaks or catches fire or spontaneously combusts, your files are still safe and accessible. If my computer exploded *right now*, I could borrow a friend's computer, log into my Dropbox account on the web, download my most recent backups, and return to work five minutes later (as long as I had a new computer to use that wasn't on fire).

Even with my files backed up this way, I store a redundant copy of all of my work (an entire folder called "Stories" roughly 1GB in size) on an external hard drive. That means the files are on my computer, on Dropbox, *and* on an external drive. Three copies is the minimum required for safety.

You can get a Dropbox account with 2GB of space for free. That's plenty of space to store a few Scrivener backups of your latest manuscript, plus some of your other files, too.

External hard drives can be purchased for less than $100 (sometimes significantly less, especially if you only need a small thumb drive) at any electronics store.

Don't tempt existential terror. Back up your work.

PART 4

For Windows

How to Write a Story in Scrivener

A Walkthrough of Scrivener's User Interface

Familiarizing Yourself with the Program

In the Scrivener walkthroughs and workshops I've done, one of the most common complaints from new users is that the interface is confusing and overwhelming. People find it difficult to get used to new software, so they give up before they even get started.

Don't worry. I'm going to walk you through the important pieces of Scrivener's interface, their names, and what each one is used for right now.

First, Install Scrivener

In order to get the most out of this book, download and install Scrivener on your computer and follow along as we explore the program.[23]

Take advantage of the thirty-day free trial or buy the program for a one-time fee of $40.

Windows Versus Mac

One more note before we get to the walkthrough: For the most part, the functionality of Scrivener for Mac and Scrivener for Windows is comparable, but there are a few notable differences.

This is the Windows tutorial, and uses screenshots on the Windows 10 operating system.

If you're on a Mac, jump over to the Mac version of the tutorial.

Project Templates

Now, let's get started!

The first screen you'll see when you open Scrivener is Project Templates. From here, you can create a blank project, start a project based on an existing template, or open a recent project.

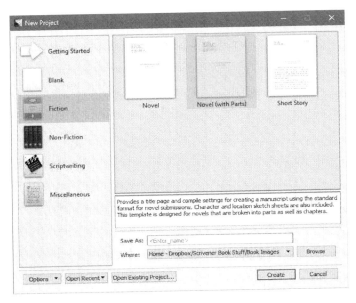

For now, open a blank project to follow along. I'll talk more about templates and teach you how to create your own when I introduce my No Nonsense Novel Template later on.

SCRIVENER SUPERPOWERS

Blank Project

This is what a blank new project in Scrivener looks like. You'll see an identical screen if you are following along.

Menu

The Menu is where you can find a full list of actions and functions, whether that's adding links and images to documents, printing, compiling, formatting, etc.

I like to spend some time with any new piece of software familiarizing myself with the Menus because they're *always* different, and always very powerful.

Don't just look at the actions, but try to perform each one. If you can't figure out what an action does, there's a handy (but dense) Scrivener Manual that you can search. Find this by going to **Help > Scrivener Manual** in the Menu.

Binder

The Binder is the left-most area of the interface. Its job is to contain all of the documents and folders in your project.

149

While most new projects give you a basic Binder structure to start with, it is completely customizable. The structure pictured above is what you will see if you open a new project using the novel template that comes with Scrivener.

The Binder is one of Scrivener's greatest advantages over other word processing software because it allows you to quickly and easily jump between sections of your manuscript, research, and other folders with scene-level granularity.

Toolbar

The Toolbar is the gray bar across the top of the program where common actions are located.

The screenshot above is the default configuration on Windows, but you can customize the Toolbar by adding and removing buttons. Simply go to **Tools > Customize Toolbars > Main Toolbar** to check out the additional buttons and options.

Inspector

The Inspector is the menu on the right hand side. Open and close it by clicking the Inspector button (the blue "i" in the circle) at the far right of the default Toolbar.

Within the Inspector, you can switch between several panes using the buttons at the top of the Inspector area. From left to right, these panes are named:

- Notes
- References
- Keywords
- Custom Meta-Data

- Snapshots
- Comments & Footnotes

In Notes, the first pane, I use everything. I use the Synopsis pane to write a summary of the scene I'm working on, the Labels and Status to label and set the status of each file of a draft. I also use the Document Notes section to take notes while I'm writing, as a kind of scene-specific scratch pad. Each document you create in Scrivener has a Synopsis and Notes section as pictured above.

Then we have the Snapshots pane. This is a crucial tool for me during the revision process. I take snapshots at the end of each draft so that I have rollback points saved in case I screw something up, change my mind, or dislike the edits I made for whatever reason.

Finally, here's a screenshot of the Comments pane. This is for leaving comments within your manuscript. To insert a comment, use the **Format > Comment** action in the Menu, click the Comment button in the Toolbar (after you add it to the Toolbar), or use the shortcut **Shift+F4**.

Explore the other panes, Custom Meta-Data and Keywords, if you want to, but don't worry about them too much. Personally, I rarely use them.

Editor

The Editor is the important part in the middle, the blank page that you write in. This is where you make words and create your stories, and where you'll be spending most of your time.

There are other view options as well, such as showing a Ruler at the top of the Editor so you can adjust tabs and margins. Do whatever makes you happy. Play around with it! The Editor, too, is completely customizable, so you can make the background bright pink if you want to.

Group/View Mode

These three buttons in the toolbar are called the "Group Mode" (when viewing a group of documents) or "View Mode" (when viewing an individual document) buttons.

They allow you to seamlessly switch between seeing your documents and subdocuments in the Editor. From left to right they are called Scrivenings ("View the document/group of documents"), Corkboard ("View the document's subdocuments on the corkboard"), or Outliner ("View the document's subdocuments in the outliner") viewing modes.

If you want to see what a button does, hover your mouse over it for a few seconds and read the text that pops up.

These are the most powerful buttons in Scrivener because they allow you to toggle between perspectives of your manuscript, another one of Scrivener's big advantages over linear, single-column word processing programs.

Scrivenings

Use the Group/View Mode button on the left to get to the Scrivenings view. This is your default view.

SCRIVENER SUPERPOWERS

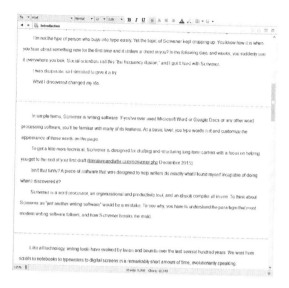

If you click on a single document in the Binder in this view, you'll be shown the text in that document within the Editor. If you click on a folder, you'll be shown the text of all files within that folder in order, with marks delineating where one file ends and another begins.

Corkboard

The middle Group/View Mode button brings up the Corkboard view.

The Corkboard is used to simulate the experience of a real-life corkboard. You can organize and edit multiple documents using a card-based interface. The size of the cards can also be changed. While it doesn't have the infinite flexibility of a real-life corkboard, I find that the digital Corkboard is faster to use, especially if you're making large structural changes.

You might outline a story using the notecards, rearrange the order of scenes by dragging and dropping them, or view all of your sketches in one place for a high-level overview. Fill the front of the index cards with text, or replace the text with an image.

Outliner

The last Group/View Mode button brings you to the Outliner, which allows you to see all your documents and metadata in a structured list.

View your entire manuscript in the Outliner, or drill down into a specific folder for a narrower view.

The columns and data you see in the screenshot above are completely customizable. Add or remove columns by clicking on the arrow to the right of the column headings and selecting the new column you'd like to add from the list that appears. You can also find these options under the Menu by going to **View > Outliner Columns** in the Menu.

That concludes our tour! Are you feeling a little better now? I hope learning the vocabulary and seeing the interface broken down into its component parts makes you feel more comfortable in the program. There's a lot to get used to for a new user, so I suggest taking a little time to explore the interface on your own. Get acquainted with the Binder and the Toolbar, especially, so that you can follow along in the next chapters.

How to Structure Your Story

Why Structure Matters

In the blank project you created to follow along during the walkthrough, direct your attention to the Binder on the left hand side. Here you'll create and organize your story and all material related to its development, such as sketches, outlines, research, drafts, and anything else you wish to keep track of.

The Binder is one of the primary advantages of using Scrivener, and it's the feature that convinces many writers to make the transition to the program from other writing software. The Binder is your writing desk. It allows you to keep all of your work in one place, stay organized with folders and subfolders, and access your work quickly when you need it.

Bird's-Eye View

Another benefit of the Binder is that it gives you a bird's-eye view of your story.

Most word processors don't have a feature that supplies this kind of visual. Instead, a writer must resort to drawing the story structure by hand, stacking sticky notes or index cards, or using a spreadsheet to lay it out. If the structure changes, as it often does while drafting, extra work must be done to maintain that diagram. Scrivener automates this process with the Binder. If you break down your manuscript correctly (which we'll cover in a moment), you'll be able to visualize the story with a glance at the Binder. Scenes will be nested into chapters and chapters into parts, according to how your story is structured.

A bird's-eye view of structure in the Binder empowers you to spot structural issues early on. Once you know your story, you'll be able to tell where the key moments are (inciting incident, first plot point, climax, resolution, etc.) and whether they fall in the right place to ensure genre-appropriate pacing. If part two of your book seems sluggish, you might look at your Binder and notice that there are significantly more scenes in part two than there are in part one, part three, or part four. Other obvious storytelling problems such as a climax that comes too early or a resolution that drags on too long are also apparent once you know what to look for in the Binder.

To give a specific example, when I finished the rough draft of my first novel I got some editorial feedback indicating in no uncertain terms that my male point-of-view character had an incomplete story. Sure enough, when I analyzed my draft in the Binder, he had fewer scenes and fewer chapters than my female point-of-view character. I hadn't realized this obvious issue while I was writing the draft, but my readers did. And there it was, plain as day, in the Binder. If I had been using a traditional word processor with no Binder, it would have been much harder to accept. With the visual in front of me, it was easy to evaluate the criticism objectively and take steps to fix the problem.

Required Folders in the Binder

There are three required folders in every Scrivener project.

1. The **Draft** or **Manuscript** folder, which contains all of the chapters and scenes that comprise your story. Consider anything in this folder officially "on the page." Everything you type in there will be Compiled in the final book file by default.

2. The **Research** folder is one of an unlimited number of containers where you store project-related information.

Nothing in this folder (or any other folder) goes into the final book file by default.

3. The **Trash** is where files go when you delete them. You can empty the trash if you wish to remove these files permanently. Once you empty the trash, there's no undo button.

You can't delete these folders, but you may rename them.

The Binder Is Yours to Command

While a default research folder is included in every Scrivener project, there's no requirement to stuff all your work in there. Create as many new folders and files as you need and organize them however you please.

I like to have separate folders for Research, Characters, and Settings at the very least. I invariably add new folders as the need arises. Here are some examples of other folders I keep in my Binder: cut scenes, old drafts, sales copy and keywords, brainstorming lists, to-do lists, front matter, series arcs, freewriting, ideas, etc.

I've done enough work in Scrivener that I like to start with a set of common folders. You can see what that looks like for me by checking out my No Nonsense Novel Template.

How to Structure Your Manuscript Folder

There's no right or wrong way to structure your research and development folders. There are, however, best practices when it comes to structuring your Manuscript folder.

To get a firm grasp on how Scrivener is supposed to be structured, we have to go back to a basic structural principle of storytelling.

SCRIVENER SUPERPOWERS

Scenes Are the Basic Unit of Storytelling

Veteran editor and writer Shawn Coyne, author of *The Story Grid: What Good Editors Know*, writes that the basic unit of storytelling is the scene: "While it can be broken down into its component beats, the scene is the most obvious mini-story."

Scrivener is also designed using the concept of the scene as the basic unit of storytelling. The program works best when you break your stories out so that each scene is in its own file, and those scenes are arranged into sections/chapter folders which roll up into part folders. That way, when you're ready to compile, your Manuscript folder is already structured to take full advantage of the Compiler.

How to Structure a Novel

Many novels abide by a simple structure. A number of chapters containing one or more scenes are arranged in order. If your story is using this simple novel structure, your Manuscript folder will be arranged like this:

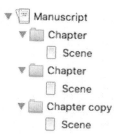

The way you title your chapter folders will be important during the final Compile process. For instance, you can tell the Compiler to name your chapters based on what you titled your chapter folders. Traditionally, the titles of scenes are left out, so you can simply number them. However, I name them with a simple sentence, like "hero meets villain," so that I know what they contain. You'll thank yourself for naming your scenes later if you end up moving them around while you're revising.

How to Structure a Novel with Parts

A more complex novel will follow the simple novel structure, except those chapters will be arranged into larger containers called parts. If you are writing a novel with parts, use this structure.

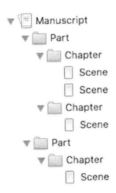

Again, as a best practice, name your part and chapter folders how you want them to appear in the final book file. You can number the chapters automatically during the compile process, or choose to use or not use the names of the chapters, parts, and scenes according to your needs. Naming them now will make it easier for you to navigate your book during the writing process.

How to Structure a Nonfiction Manuscript with Parts

A nonfiction manuscript with parts is similar to a novel with parts. Here's an example of a nonfiction manuscript generated using the Non-Fiction (with Parts) template that comes packaged with Scrivener.

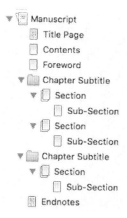

In this example, there are several documents that appear in the manuscript before the first chapter begins, and an endnotes file as well. If your book is structured like this, check out the Non-Fiction (with Parts) template to get you started.

How This Book Is Structured

Like the previous example, the book you're reading is a nonfiction book with multiple parts. Here's how the first couple parts of this book appear in the Binder:

- Front Matter
- Manuscript
  - Introduction
    - Scrivener Superpowers
      - Rock Bottom
      - What Is Scrivener?
      - The Next Evolutionary Stage of Writing Software
      - The Lightbulb Moment
    - The Main Benefits of Scrivener
      - Get Organized
      - Amplify Your Productivity
      - Take Your Writing Across the Finish Line
  - Interviews with Authors
    - Conversations about Scriveners
      - Garrett Robinson
      - Gwen Hernandez
      - Joanna Penn
      - Joe Bunting
      - Rachel Aaron
      - Simon Whistler

Notice how the nesting dictates where the parts are, where the subheadings are, and where the sections are. Unlike a novel, where I only use the chapter names, for nonfiction books I rely on the names of the documents to generate the subheadings in the final book file.

Where to Put Front and Back Matter

In the screenshot above you'll also see that I have a Front Matter folder.

Front matter is anything that comes before the beginning of your story: a title page, copyright, table of contents, etc. Front matter goes in a separate folder outside the Manuscript folder. Many templates generate front matter templates for you, so I'd recommend opening a few new projects using the templates Scrivener provides and checking them out. During the Compile process (which we'll cover in detail in a later chapter) you can choose which folder/file to use as the front matter for your compiled book.

Back matter is a bit different. To have files appear at the end of your manuscript, like calls-to-action, teasers of your next book, and your author bio, you have to place those folders inside the Manuscript folder after the last chapter of your book. There's no place in the Compile process to select what to include as your back matter.

Structure Smart

Break your story down by scene, arrange those scenes into their containing chapters and those chapters into their containing parts, and you'll be prepared for revisions and the Compiling process later. Not only that, but you'll automate the diagramming of your story structure and be able to spot problems with your manuscript early.

How to Create Character Sketches

How do you create compelling characters?

Nothing is born in a vacuum. Characters don't emerge fully formed. Creating compelling characters is a process of getting to know them and working to make them come to life. They're developed through character sketches, through the writing process itself, through lots feedback, and through diligent revision.

What Is a Character Sketch?

Think of a character sketch as the rough draft of your character. It's a place where you can freely experiment, where you can tell yourself who your characters are, how they look, and where they come from.

You can type out their whole backstory or just the parts of the timeline that inform your character's identity. Their inner and external conflicts will be crucial to your story, so be sure to include those, too.

Most importantly, use character sketches as a tool to discover your characters' key motivations and goals, because they are the engine that drive your story forward.

How to Use Template Sheets in Scrivener

Scrivener has Template Sheets that make building out character sketches easy. If you started using one of their document templates, like the novel template that comes with Scrivener or my No Nonsense Novel Template, there should already be a Template Sheets folder in the your project document that looks like this screenshot:

If not, you can make a Template Sheets folder by creating a new folder in the Binder, selecting it, and then from the Menu choosing **Project > Set Selection as Templates Folder**.

Visualize Your Characters Using Scrivener's Corkboard

Now that you have your Template Sheets folder set up, you can generate character sketches by creating new files from the Template Sheets you've created.

There are two ways to do this. In the Toolbar, click the arrow next to the Add button, go to **New From Template**, then click on the template you wish to create. Or, right click on the folder you wish to add a new sketch to in the Binder, then go to **Add > New From Template > Name of Your Template**.

Here's the cast of characters from an early draft of my first novel:

SCRIVENER SUPERPOWERS

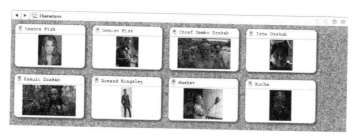

I go for visuals out of the gate, as it helps me ground my character in an image. Having a photo in front of me makes writing about them easier, at first, because the photos jog my imagination. Once I really know my characters (i.e. about twenty-five percent of the way through the first draft), I don't need to look at the visuals at all. By that point I have a more vivid image of the characters in my head.

If you can't find photos for every character, that's okay. Remember that nothing about your planning or pre-production phase (to borrow a film term) is set in stone. Your story will evolve as you write, and so will your characters.

For the images, I've picked a few photos I found online. There are several excellent resources on the Internet to get free stock photos.

Here are some of my favorites:
- Unsplash
- Wikimedia Commons
- Pexels
- Pixabay
- MorgueFile[10]

To add a photo to a Character Sketch in Scrivener, open your character's notecard and find the Notes pane of the Inspector. Change the Synopsis pane to take an image by using the switcher in the top right of the Synopsis frame (the little orange graphic with double arrows next to it in the screenshot below), then drag your image into the black image area where you can see the phrase "Drag an image file":

To insert a photo inline with the text of your sketch, first click where you want the photo, and then go to **Edit > Insert > Image from File...**

You can also drag and drop photos into the Editor to accomplish the same task.

Individual Character Sketches

Here's a screenshot of an individual sketch of one of my characters:

This sketch was created using the Character Sketch Template Sheet that comes with Scrivener. I've since abandoned Scrivener's defaults in favor of my own compilation, which follows.

An Alternative Character Sketch Template

As you learn more about character sketches, you'll probably want to customize your character sketch template and make it your own. Personally, I find Scrivener's default sketch sheets superficial. When sketching characters, I like less structure and fewer prescriptive fields concerning the character's physical appearance and personality.

This is my preferred character sketch, the same one I include in my No Nonsense Novel Template. Here's what it looks like in Scrivener:

And here's the full text, which you can feel free to use or modify as you see fit:

[photo]

FULL NAME

One Sentence Synopsis
This character in a single sentence.

Summary
This is a paragraph summary of your character. Include physical attributes, habits, mannerisms. Sketch your character.

Motivations & Goals
What do they want?

Conflicts
What makes them human?

Narrative
What happens to them in the story? What else is important?

Why Character Sketches Work

There are practical reasons to do character sketches. For one, developing characters is a process. Starting with character sketches is a great way to give the gel of your ideas time and space to set.

Yes, they're extra effort, and yes, they can be difficult. But that's part of the process.

If you feel like you really know the character and are ready to move on, run through this checklist to double check your work:

SCRIVENER SUPERPOWERS

1. What is your character's primary motivation?
2. How does your character change through the course of the story?
3. What does your character look like?
4. How does your character act around their parents? Their friends? Their boss?
5. How does your character respond under stress?
6. What is your character's weakness, their kryptonite?
7. What will your character die for?
8. What is your character's biggest hypocrisy?
9. Who are your character's friends?

If you can answer all of these questions with confidence, congratulations, you're ready for setting sketches, which are covered in the next section.

How to Create Setting Sketches

"If character is the foreground of fiction, setting is the background," Janet Burroway tells the reader in *Writing Fiction: A Guide to Narrative Craft*. But how do you create engaging settings that enhance your story? And how can Scrivener help you create setting sketches for your particular story?

People (and therefore characters) are a product of their environment, for good or for ill. In order to write compelling stories that draw readers in, you not only have to know your setting intimately, but be able to manipulate that setting to bring out the best and worst in your characters.

A good setting can take on personality traits of its own, and some tend to think of setting as another character.[11]

All settings have to start somewhere. Let's go over a classic method to help you flesh out your settings early in the process so that they can become a vital part of your story.

What Is a Setting Sketch?

A setting sketch is an outline of a fictional place—what it looks like, smells like, feels like. You can discuss a setting objectively through the lens of your own experiences, or you can take the same setting and examine it through the eyes of a character.

Settings also create atmosphere and tone in your story. Horror stories are great examples of effective setting because they create an atmosphere of fear that is almost palpable; it's what makes them such gripping stories, whether you're working with a haunted house, a zombie apocalypse, or a ruined castle.

As with character sketches, I like to start with visuals using Scrivener's Corkboard.

Character or Setting Sketch—Which Comes First?

In the last chapter, we talked about how character sketches can help you flesh out the characters in your story, so you might be wondering: Which should you work on first, your character sketches or your setting sketches?

Both character and setting sketches are fundamental to the planning phase of the creative writing process, but the order in which you tackle them is your choice.

I'm of the mindset that you can do setting, character, or plot in any order that makes the most sense to you. Play to your own strengths.

Don't worry too much about what you do first. Over time, you will develop your own process, and adjust these tactics and tools to fit your style.

Using Template Sheets in Scrivener for Setting Sketches

As with character sketches, you'll want to use the Template Sheets for setting sketches.

Visualize Your Settings

Start by creating a folder called "Settings." Then open that folder to the Corkboard view and create a notecard for each setting in your story using Template Sheets, the same way we did for character sketches in the last chapter. As a reminder, you can either right click on the folder and go to **Add > New From Template** and select your setting sketch, or click the arrow next to the **Add** button in the Toolbar to add new sketches.

If your whole story takes place in one room in one house, you might have only a single card. More likely though, your story takes place in multiple settings.

Try to be as specific as possible. Instead of "New York City," name your card "The Village" or, even better, "Italian Restaurant in the Village." The more specific your setting, the more likely it is to come to life.

Once you have all your setting notecards arranged, go find one image that feels like it matches each setting. There can be discrepancies between the details of the photo you choose and the actual setting in your story. The idea isn't to find a photo that represents your story in every way possible, but to capture the spirit of that particular setting so you have a place to start your sketch.

Here are the setting cards I created for my novel:

If you find it necessary to use more than one photo, you can add extra images inside the Scrivenings view of a particular sketch.

Write About Your Setting

Now for the fun part: open up a setting and start writing.

Here's a screenshot of what the default Template Sheet for a setting sketch looks like in Scrivener. I've filled it out with one of the settings in my novel.

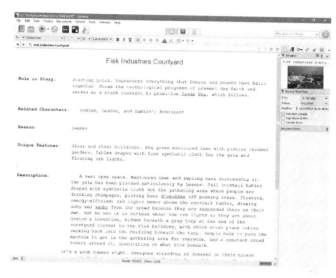

Aim for at least 500 words. Any more than that is icing on the cake. Any less than that and you may find yourself coming back to the sketch to flesh it out more as you write. Better to have it and not need it than the other way around.

An Alternative Setting Sketch Template

Here's an alternative setting sketch template you may use in your writing practice. This is my preferred setting sketch.

What I like about this version, compared to Scrivener's default, is that it's less prescriptive. It leaves room for the imagination to run wild, cuing you with suggestions rather than specific questions. For example, you see in the default sketch above, the label "season"? All I wrote there was "summer." That wasn't important to my story, so it was really just a waste of a label. In my sketch, I've combined "Weather & Seasons," as I find that there is a lot of information to mine with both those categories, whereas a season alone isn't very significant in the stories I want to tell.

You have plenty of room to experiment here, so mix and match until you find what works for you.

Here's the full text of my setting sketch. Feel free to use or modify it as you see fit:

[photo]

SETTING NAME

Role in Story
This setting in a single sentence.

Related Characters
Character A, Character B, Character C.

Description
Describe your setting in significant detail.

Weather & Season
Windy, rainy, gloomy, sunny, clear, foggy, humid, altitude, storms? Summer, spring, fall, winter?

Sights, Sounds & Smells
Use your senses and go there. Sketch out what aspects of your setting are most important to your character, what they look like, smell like, how the characters feel when they see this place.

Details
Anything else important to remember?

Setting Sketch Checklist

How do you know when your setting sketch is done? That depends on your own unique process. You're done when you can't squeeze any more juice out of the setting you're working on.

Just in case you're still not sure, here's a checklist you can run through that may help you out. Consider each of your setting sketches and ask yourself the following questions:

1. What unique atmosphere does this setting evoke?

2. What important role does this setting play in my story?

3. Would my story be the same if I changed this setting? Why or why not?

4. Go through the weather patterns: rain, wind, snow, hot, cold, humid—what about this setting is consistent in each type of weather? What about this setting is inconsistent?

5. What year is it in this setting? Why does that matter?

6. How does this setting influence each of my characters?

How to Storyboard Your Story

Storyboarding is the process of mapping out your story, often using index cards, in a high-level way that allows you to see your story visually and rearrange it.

Scrivener's Corkboard provides the perfect interface to storyboard your novel digitally.

When Should You Storyboard?

The storyboarding process can be undertaken at any phase in the writing of a story. Storyboarding is a tool I use several times during the writing process: before I begin writing (i.e. planning/plotting), during the rough draft (when I get stuck), and when I'm revising. It's a way to see the big picture, make sure your story has good bones, and ensure that everything flows logically from one scene to the next.

It's also the tool that allows you to combine the work you've done for the previous three chapters: your knowledge of how to structure your manuscript, your characters, and your settings. Your storyboard is where they all come together. Having characters, settings, and an idea of your plot in mind ahead of time will make the storyboarding process much simpler.

SCRIVENER SUPERPOWERS

How to Create Your Storyboard in Scrivener

Follow these steps to storyboard in Scrivener:

1. **To Begin, Create a New Folder.**
   Move the new folder outside of the Manuscript section of the Binder. Call this folder "Storyboard."

2. **View the Folder as a Corkboard.**
   After you create your new storyboarding folder, open it, and view it as a Corkboard (background color/style varies depending on your settings):

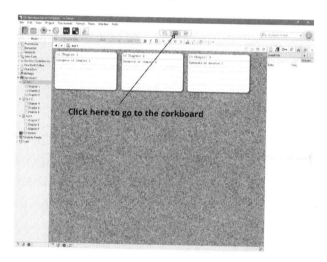

3. **Create Index Cards for the Major Sections of Your Book.** Next, create an index card for your first act or chapter. To do this, just create a new document, as you normally would for a new scene or chapter, within the Storyboard folder. When you use the Corkboard view, these documents will automatically become index cards. I'll let you start as big as you want. Sometimes, I'll

start planning (especially in the early phase of idea generation) with only three or four cards, one for each "act."

Sometimes I start with a "beginning" card and an "end" card.

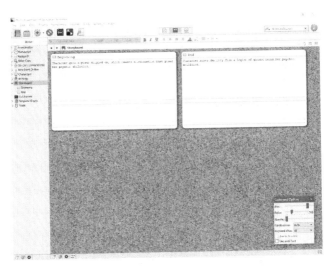

There's no right or wrong way.

Let's say you've thought about it for a while and have a vague idea of how your chapters should be laid out. Great. Create a card and write the title of the chapter at the top of the card.

Even if you don't plan to title your chapters in the final story, use titles as an exercise in specificity. Maybe you're writing a literary story and you want those fancy roman numerals to head each chapter, or you don't want chapter breaks at all, just a blank space between sections like Frank McCourt uses in Angela's Ashes. That's fine. Challenge yourself to title your sections anyway. This isn't the final result, but an exercise in getting to know your story better.

SCRIVENER SUPERPOWERS

In the body of the card, write a one or two sentence description of the main purpose of the chapter, like I've done in the screenshot above. The goal here is to get to the point. Often, I don't know what the main purpose of my chapter is and I'll have to think really hard about it. Sometimes I delete a chapter entirely. Other times I break a chapter into two because there are two important points I want to hit. In both cases, the story is stronger for it.

Once you're done with the first chapter card, create a new index card for the second, third, fourth, etc. until you've reached the end of your story. It's that simple, but unless you're an experienced storyteller—and perhaps even if you are—it won't be easy.

4. **Create Index Cards for Each Scene**

   Once your first round of cards is complete, it's time to go deeper into your story. If you started with acts, break them down into chapters. If you began with chapters, whittle them down into scenes. Challenge yourself to be as specific as possible.

   Scenes are the basic unit of storytelling, as we've discussed, so your goal is to get down to the scene level.
   If you write those short one-scene chapters like Dan Brown or David Baldacci, you're in luck: that's as deep as you need to go. Keep in mind that not everyone writes that way. Often, books have multiple scenes within each chapter, so keep breaking your index cards down until you have a card for each scene.

   At this point, you might have to make an organizational decision. You can nest your scenes within your chapters (or your chapters within your acts), which will require a lot of hopping up and down levels to view the cards you've created across the whole story, but which will show fewer cards on the screen at any given time. Or you can keep them all on one screen. Here's an example three-act story structure with three chapters in each act, opened to Act I. As you can see, when you're viewing Act I, you're limited to seeing just the cards within the selected folder.

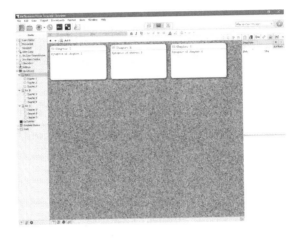

If you're writing an epic fantasy novel, I would understand if you wanted to nest your chapters and scenes within larger containers like this. Storyboard one act at a time to make it less overwhelming.

Next, when we transition to a physical medium, you'll be able to get a big picture view.

5. Print Out Your Storyboard

You would need several screens to get a good bird's-eye view of your story on the computer. Fortunately, now that you've begun to storyboard in Scrivener, you can transition to a physical version very easily. All you need is a printer and a pair of scissors

While you're in the Corkboard view, go to File > Print Current Document... and print out the digital notecards you've created. Scrivener will print these with dotted borders around each card.

Now, it's arts and crafts day in school! Grab a pair of scissors and cut the paper into individual index cards. Then use an actual corkboard with pushpins—or the floor, or a long piece of butcher paper—to lay it all out.

I used this process when I was rewriting my novel *The Auriga Project*. Here's what my story looks like on a physical corkboard. Each card is a scene, and each group of cards represents a chapter.

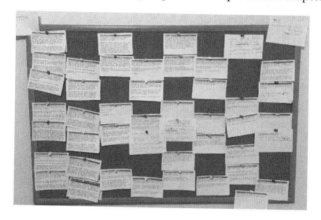

One note of warning: if your description within the body of the index card in Scrivener is too long, the text will overflow to multiple cards when you print it out. If that happens, pare back your description or simply stack the cards after you cut them out.

This step isn't strictly necessary. I don't usually print out my storyboard until I'm on my second or third draft and I need a way to see the story with fresh eyes. Again, you'll develop your own process. Do what's best for you.

Corkboard Settings

This is a good time to point out some Corkboard settings. Using the button in the bottom right of the Corkboard interface, you can change the size, ratio, spacing, and arrangement of your Corkboard.

You can find additional settings for the Corkboard in the Menu under **View > Corkboard Options**.

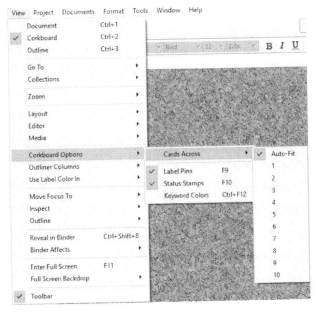

Finally, it's worth pointing out that the colors in the photo of my physical Corkboard came through because of the labels I applied to my scenes. I created labels for each point-of-view character (blue for the male lead, green for the female lead). You can turn on label colors by going to **View > Use Label Color In** and selecting where you want the colors to show. This comes through when you print them out, which has a nice visual effect. I'll go into more detail about labels in the chapter on Metadata.

Four Storyboarding Questions

Now that you can see your story as a whole in a physical medium, rearrange it and move cards around. Don't be afraid to mess it up, because your work is already saved in Scrivener at the point you printed it out. I find that seeing my story in a physical medium will reveal flaws I missed or couldn't see on a smaller computer screen.

Here are a few questions to ask yourself at this phase:

1. **Does each scene have a purpose?** If you remove a scene from your storyboard, what happens to your story? Make sure each scene contributes to the story in a meaningful way by revealing a new piece of information, developing your characters, and/or bringing your protagonist closer to (or farther from) their goal.

2. **Does your plot have continually rising action?**[13] Your story should have continually rising action so that the plot never goes slack or bores the reader. Read more about rising action online.

3. **Is there a consistent timeline?** Make sure that your timelines all match up, especially if you have multiple point-of-view characters. If your timeline is complex or difficult to keep track of, consider mapping it out in another tool called Aeon Timeline.[14] They also supply specific documentation for integrating Aeon Timeline with Scrivener.[15]

4. **Have you hit all the important plot points?** You need an inciting incident, several scenes with rising action, a first plot point/doorway of no return, a second plot point/doorway of no return, a climax, and a resolution (at a minimum). Refer to the story craft books listed in the

further reading recommendations if these terms for key story moments aren't familiar to you.

If you look closely at the photograph of my corkboard for *The Auriga Project*, you'll notice a couple edits that I made at this phase in the process. Can you spot them?

I added three scenes (and removed a few others). Don't take this step for granted!

Then Make Changes in Scrivener

Once you've rearranged your story physically and you are happy with it, copy any changes you made back into Scrivener. I know this part is tedious, but keep in mind that all this work will make your story stronger—and make it easier for you to write it (or rewrite it!) when you are done.

Now, Start Writing Your Draft!

Finally, you're ready to start drafting. If you used this storyboarding process to outline a story you haven't yet written, here's what you do: duplicate your storyboard and drag the copy into the Manuscript folder of the Binder. If you haven't already done so, arrange the scenes into chapter containers.

Since you worked so hard to break the story out into scenes, your Manuscript is already arranged according to the best practices for structure in Scrivener that we covered earlier. You can then simply open the first scene and start typing. The description you wrote on the front of the index cards appears in the Synopsis section (top of the Notes pane in the Inspector), which makes it easy to reference while you're drafting.

The reason I suggest moving a copy of the storyboard you made instead of dragging the original over is that your story is going to continue to evolve as you write it. It's educational to compare the story you actually write to the storyboard you prepared once your draft is complete.

If, however, you used storyboarding to help you get unstuck or to revise your story at the end of a draft, you'll have to update your Manuscript folder to match your new outline. That means deleting scenes, moving scenes around, rearranging chapters, etc. Again, keep a copy of your storyboard for comparison later.

How to Start and Finish a Draft

You're Ready to Start Drafting

At this point, you've been introduced to the important pieces of Scrivener's user interface; you know how to structure your book; you know how to create character and setting sketches using Template Sheets; and you have a complete account of my storyboarding process for planning and getting unstuck while you're writing.

In other words, you have all the tools you need to start drafting.

Editor Settings

The blank page in the middle of Scrivener where you write your story, also called the Editor, is highly customizable. Before you begin, take a second to adjust your Editor settings. You'll be spending a lot of time here, so make sure everything is just how you like it.

You can manage the Editor Preferences by going to **Tools > Options** in the Menu and adjusting the options in the Editor and Appearance panes.

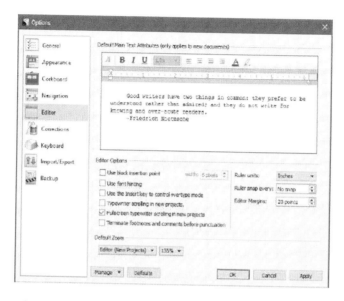

If you like to have a Ruler and Format Bar visible, you can hide/show those in the Menu under **Format > Ruler** and **Format > Format Bar**. I always have these showing so that I can adjust margins, alignment, and spacing quickly.

Use settings that please you during the writing phase, because a happy writer is a productive writer. But also be aware that when you get to the compile phase, *you'll specify different formatting settings with Compile*. In other words, there is one group of settings that affects your Editor, and another group of settings that affects the formatting of the final document you generate with Compile. So if you want to write with blue Comic Sans text on a camouflage background, more power to you. That does *not* mean that those Editor formatting choices will carry over to your ebook or print book. We'll go over Compile in depth in a later chapter.

Full Screen Composition Mode

Did you know that Scrivener also has a distraction-free Full Screen mode? There should be a button in your Toolbar that looks like a black square with white arrows pointing at opposite corners of the square. When you hover your mouse over this icon, it will say "Enter Full Screen." Click that button to enter Full Screen mode or go to the Menu to find it: **View > Enter Full Screen**. Lastly, you can use the hotkey **F11**.

Full Screen mode is a great way to write when you want to eliminate distractions and focus on your work.

To change the settings of the Full Screen mode, go to the Appearance pane in your Options. In the Menu, go to **Tools > Options > Appearance**, then find the Full Screen list under Colors:

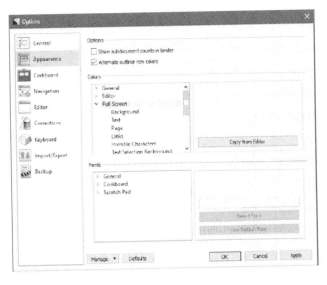

Just like the Editor, Full Screen is fully customizable. None of these settings will be reflected in your ebook when you compile, so adjust it to your heart's content.

In Full Screen, you can still access your Inspector panes and make other adjustments using the toolbar at the bottom of the screen. If it's not visible, hover your mouse at the bottom of the screen until it pops up.

You may also change the background of Full Screen mode. I suggest uploading a photo of something relaxing, like a beach or forest or other natural landscape. To upload a new background photo go to **View > Full Screen Backdrop > Choose...** and pick a photo from your computer. Then adjust the Background Fade toggle in the Full Screen toolbar (bottom right of your screen) so that the photo isn't distracting.

To exit Full Screen mode, click the double arrows on the right of the Full Screen toolbar, or press Escape on your keyboard.

Notes, Comments, and Annotations

While you're writing, use the Document Notes, Comments, and Inline Annotations features to mark issues for fixing later. This allows you to get a thought down without interrupting the creative flow state you enter while drafting. Don't resolve any of these comments, notes or annotations now. You'll come back to them during your first revision, *after* the draft is complete.

Here are the three types of comments/notes in Scrivener and how to use them.

Document Notes

There is a unique Document Notes section available for each text file and folder in the Binder. You can find it at the bottom of the Notes pane of the Inspector.

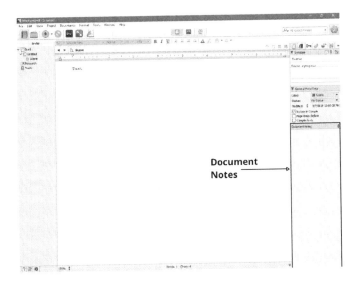

Document Notes

There's no right or wrong way to use this piece of the interface. When I first started using Scrivener, I had no idea what I would put there. Now, I fill it with all sorts of information about the scene I'm writing: How I feel about the scene, what's missing, a different way to approach the scene, what I like about it, a reminder to look up a piece of technology or do research on a topic, an idea for another scene, and even ideas for new stories.

Comments

Comments have their own pane of the Inspector. You can add a comment to your text by going to **Format > Comment** in the Menu, or using the shortcut **Shift+F4**.

The benefit of using this feature, as opposed to making a note in the Document Notes section, is that clicking on the comment takes you to the comment's place in your text, so it's easy to use comments to jump around your manuscript.

Inline Annotations

The third commenting feature is called Inline Annotations. Adding an Inline Annotation turns the annotated text red and draws a red box around it. This makes the annotation stick out like a sore thumb, and I use them for anything I don't know yet—for instance, characters or places that need a name (or need to be re-named). I might also use Inline Annotations on any phrasing that is questionable but which I don't have time or brainpower to work through at the moment.

```
Character name was playing basketball with his friends.
When all of a sudden...
Boom! A meteorite struck the apartment building down the street.
```

Say you want to use the name of a city your characters have traveled to, but you haven't named the city yet—perhaps you just invented it. To prevent interrupting your flow, hit the shortcut **Ctrl+Shift+A** for Inline Annotation, type "Name of city" (it will appear in red in your Editor like the screenshot above), and simply move on. The annotation will remind you that you need to fix it later when you come across it during the revision phase. That way, you're marking the issue to be fixed without interrupting your productivity.

Storyboard If You Get Stuck

If you come up against a block or a particularly sticky plot issue that you can't plow through, take a step back and return to your storyboard. Ask yourself why you stopped writing and brainstorm ways to fix the problem.

When I get stuck during drafting, I'll first pick up my notebook and a pen and start journaling about the problem I've run into to find the core issue that caused my dilemma. Whether you like to write by hand when you do this or you prefer to type, I recommend doing this *outside* of Scrivener because the change of surroundings (and medium) will spark connections in your brain and give you a break from pounding your head against the same wall.

Once you identify what the problem is, revise your storyboard until you've found an effective fix to the problem.

When you are happy with your storyboard again or you have pinpointed the issue, make those changes in Scrivener and carry on writing.

Start Writing!

All right, no more procrastination. You've done the necessary planning. All that's left is to put words on the page.

Get a cup of coffee or tea. Take a deep breath—or three.

Now put your butt in that chair and start typing.

How to Set Targets and Measure Your Progress

As much as writing is an art, it is also a craft. It involves learned skills. And like a carpenter who can measure the dimensions of his materials, so too can writers measure the output of their work.

In other words, the craft of writing is *quantifiable*.

Every story is made up of words that you can count. *War and Peace* is roughly 250,000 words. *Of Mice and Men* is about 30,000 words. Fiction magazines typically accept short stories to a maximum of 7,000 words, depending on the publication. And their payment rates are often advertised *per word*.

In college, my professors used to assign essays based on the number of pages required. Write a ten-page essay on Shakespeare's *Hamlet*, for instance. This led to a lot of font-size and margin-adjustment cheating, thereby inadvertently putting focus on the wrong goal.

I wish they had given me word counts instead. I wish they had told me that with an average of 250 words per double spaced page, a ten-page essay is roughly the equivalent of 2,500 words. It would have made more sense to me and prevented any gaming of the system through sizing changes. It would also have given me a better sense of my rate of production as a writer and made me ask important questions earlier, like: How much effort goes into a thousand words? And how much time do you need to spend to produce that result?

Years later, when I started researching how to submit short fiction, I realized that writing was quantifiable. I started to do the math and very quickly learned that if I just got the words out every day, eventually I'd be holding a story in my hands. If I wrote

1,000 words a day, after a week I'd have a short story; after sixty days, I'd have a novel. It's that simple, and simple is manageable.

To get a sense of how to quantify a story, here are some generally accepted standards for word counts in fiction:

- Microfiction/flash fiction: Up to 1,000 words?
- Short story: 1,000 – 10,000 words
- Novelette: 10,000 – 30,000 words
- Novella: 30,000 – 50,000 words
- Novel: 50,000+ words

You can use these numbers and a good sense of your rate of production to schedule your work and measure your progress. (If you are wondering what lengths of work a certain market accepts, look at a tool like Duotrope[16] or The (Submission) Grinder[17] to research markets, find out what kind of work they accept, and learn what they pay for each accepted submission.)

So that begs the question: How do you figure out what your rate of production is?

Learn by Experimentation

Are you familiar with the scientific method? Here's a simplified version: Step one, come up with a good question. Step two, run an experiment to test your hypothesis. Step three, compare your hypothesis to the results of your experiment. Step four, create a new hypothesis based on your newly acquired knowledge, and try it again.

Writers can follow the same process. Since you work with words, your hypothesis should be pretty straightforward, but let me start you off with some basic questions to answer.

- How long does it take me to write 1,000 words?
- Am I most productive in the mornings, afternoons, evenings, or nights?
- What is a sustainable daily word count goal for me?

- How can I change my schedule to make time for writing every day?

It's really important for my own process that I keep track of my daily word count. This gives me the feeling of motion and a sense of making progress. Most importantly, keeping track of my progress teaches me more about myself and how I write.

For example, after writing the first draft of my first novel (and keeping track in my notebook of how many words I wrote each day), I learned that my average word count is around 1,000 words per day. Pretty standard, right? What I didn't expect to learn was that I can get up to 2,500 words on a really great day, but that my bad days can be in the 300 word range—or less!

What a difference this kind of knowledge would have made in my essay writing days in college. Instead of cramming ten pages into the night before an assignment was due, I would have been encouraged to spread the work out over the amount of time it would take me to write it, and set achievable milestones. Once I discovered Scrivener, I did exactly that with my fiction.

You can do the same. Here's how you can use Scrivener to set targets and measure your progress.

Project Targets in Scrivener

Scrivener's Project Targets function (**Project > Project Targets**) shows you two progress bars: one for Manuscript Target and one for Session Target.

Let's start with the more immediate one.

Session Target

The Session Target calculates how many words you typed today. By default, only words written in the compile group are included in the daily count. Typically, that includes all files in the Manuscript folder. That means any notes, outline adjustments, character sketches, setting sketches, and words typed in files stored outside of your Manuscript folder are not included in the Session Target. To include all documents in the word count, uncheck the "Documents included in compile only" box in the Project Targets window shown above.

If you're in the planning phase, you may want to consider including your research material in the count so you can measure your research production rate. You can choose whether or not to include a specific document in the compile group by navigating to the Notes section of the Inspector for any particular file and checking the "Include in Compile" checkbox.

As I mentioned earlier, my personal session target goal is usually 1,000 words on a normal day. If you're unsure of your own production rate, a thousand words per day is a good place to start. But be sure to adjust your goal fit your schedule and experience.

Manuscript Target

The other progress bar in the Project Targets screen is the Manuscript Target. Use this to set your word count target for the entire book you're currently writing.

Employ the word counts listed above for each type of fiction story to give you an idea of a general target for the type of work you're writing. If what you're writing isn't listed there, check out other books in your genre and estimate their word counts to give you a sense of the market.

My Manuscript Target is never perfect the first time. The goal is not to be exact, but to set a target to work toward. You can adjust your target as you write, so don't overthink it.

Once you decide on a number for your Manuscript Target and Session Target, type those numbers into the number fields in the Project Targets window to set them.

View Progress in the Outliner

Scrivener also makes word counts by folder and scene easily visible.

To get a holistic view of this, here's a screenshot of the Outliner view:

In order to see your work in the Outliner, click the third Group/View Mode button in the Toolbar. In the screenshot above, I'm viewing the whole manuscript, but I could click into any folder if I wanted a narrower view.

The right-hand column showing Total Word Count is not visible by default. I added it because I like to see the word count of each section of my project. To add that column to your screen, click on the arrow to the right of the column headers and select Total Word Count from the list of column options that appear.

Finally, the Progress bar in the last column shows a visual measure of your recorded word count compared to the target you've set for that file/folder. You also have to add this column to your Outliner if you'd like to see it.

Setting Targets by Scene

Scrivener gives you the ability to set the word count targets not just for your manuscript or for your current writing session, but for each section of your book as well. However you break up your story, you can estimate length and plan your production by setting targets at the scene level.

To set the word count Target of a document, open and find the Target icon in the lower right-hand corner of the Editor. Here's a close-up:

When you click on the icon, you'll be asked to set the Target for this document:

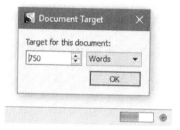

Another way to do this it to is to reveal the Target column in the Outliner view, and double click on the cell to edit the Target that way.

And that's it! Now go through and set the word count Target on each document in your outline or storyboard. When that's done, you'll be able to estimate how long your complete manuscript will be. You can use this number to set your Manuscript Target if you haven't already done so.

One warning: Scrivener's Session Target count is calculated as the net total of your words. If you type 1,000 new words, then delete 300 words, your current day's session target will read 700 words.

The daily word count is just a tool to help you keep yourself accountable. What's important is how your progress tracks over time, so be kind to yourself.

Tracking Your Progress Over Time

Unfortunately, while Scrivener does a great job of tracking your progress in your current session, and while it does an even better job of making the word count visible across your entire manuscript, it does an absolutely terrible job of tracking word count over time, let alone tracking word count across multiple projects.

We're going to have to create our own progress tracking tool that we can use on a daily basis. There's no doubt in my mind that tracking progress over time is important. It's what all your daily inputs—of any size—eventually add up to that really matter. Here are a few different options for tracking your progress over time.

You can write your daily word count in a notebook or in a Project Note in Scrivener. To use a Project Note, go to **Project > Project Notes** in the Menu, create a new note named "Word Count," and record your progress there every day.

Be sure to include *at least* the date, what you were working on, and the number of words you got down. I used this method for several months on my first novel. After I finished the rough draft, I also wrote a blog about my word count goals and results[18] for that project. Check it out to see detailed graphs of my word count progress over time as well as lessons learned.

My preferred method to store word count data, however, is a spreadsheet. I store my spreadsheet in Google Drive. The columns across the top are labeled:

- Date
- Project name
- Word count
- Time started
- Time ended
- Notes (How I felt, any problems I encountered aanything else that comes to mind)

Every day, I record what I've done in the spreadsheet and check to see how I'm tracking against my goals.

I give you these options to show you what's possible. You have to create a system and a process that works for you. Tracking words and optimizing your production is vital to the writing life. When you traffic in words, when your ability to pay the rent and put food on the table depends on your writing, why would you *not* want to keep track of your rate of production?

When Are You Most Productive?

In *2k to 10k* Rachel Aaron also suggests keeping track of the *hours* in which you write, so that you can calculate a words per hour figure. This is smart, and it's the reason I include "Start Time" and "End Time" columns in my spreadsheets.

Her reasoning is that by keeping this data, she found out what time of day was the most productive time for her (i.e. what time of day yielded the most words per hour on average). That's valuable. If you don't know when you are most creative and productive, find out.

I already know that I am most creative and productive in the morning. My mind is sharpest and the world is the quietest in the early hours. Those are *my* most productive hours, but yours might be in the afternoon, evening, or late at night. Only you will be able to tell when you're most productive, and the way you come to this conclusion is by thorough experimentation with diligently recorded results.

If your schedule is less flexible or you have to write in the margins of the day—before work, at lunch, on the train ride to work—I'd say forget this advice and write as much as you can during your writing sessions. Be sure to keep those sessions sacred and focused. Make use of the time you have.

After all, writing is simple. When you boil it down, all it takes is effort over time. That's powerful knowledge, and that knowledge will help you finish your manuscript.

How to Use Metadata and Stay Organized

Once you get into your draft, your workspace may get a little chaotic.

Embrace it. Make a mess. That's part of the creative process, and one of the benefits of using Scrivener is that you can wrangle that mess back into order at the end of your draft with relative ease. As long as you broke your story down into scenes in the planning phase like we discussed, you can drag and drop to rearrange later, and jump quickly through your story to make revisions and edits.

If you're like me, though, you'll want to have a system in place that allows for chaos without letting your story get out of control or—worse—overwhelming you. Scrivener gives you many ways to stay organized through a messy writing process.

They call it Meta-Data (though the common spelling is "metadata"). If you're not familiar with the term, metadata is a set of data that describes and gives information about other data. In the case of your book, that means data on your scenes, chapters, and other documents and folders within your book. Word count of a scene is a piece of metadata. Other metadata includes point of view (Old Man Ford, Bad Guy the Villain), setting (Old Man Ford's House, Police Station), status (To Do, First Draft, Revised Draft, Final Draft), or anything else you can come up with.

Here are several ways to stay organized with Scrivener Meta-Data and how it can make your life easier during the writing process.

Meta-Data Settings

To access the Meta-Data Settings, go to **Project > Meta-Data Settings...** in the Menu.

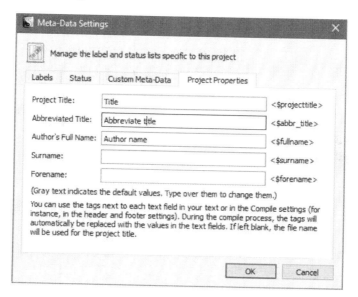

This is a screenshot of the Project Properties pane. You can change your book title and your author name here. These values will be used later when you compile your story for editing or publication.

Labels and Color Coding

The next pane is Labels. You can change the title "Label" at the top of this pane and add as many values as you like. I like to use this one for "Point of View" and name the values after my characters. The screenshot, however, shows Scrivener's defaults.

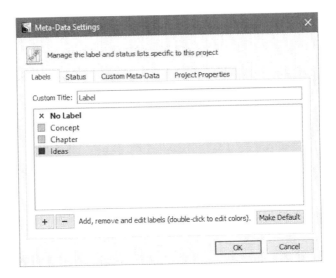

I also color-code the labels I use. This is part of the reason I like using POV as the Label, because then I can easily see in the Outliner view how many of my scenes are from each character's POV simply by their color-coded arrangement. It allows me to check at a glance where one character might be hogging the spotlight, or where another character's POV is missing from an important part of the book. Here's what *The Auriga Project* looks like in the Binder with POV color-coding:

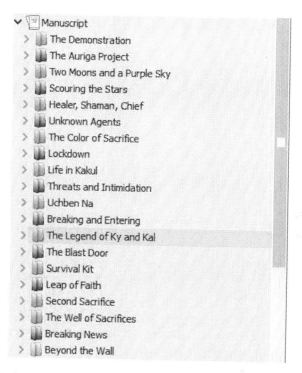

You have to turn the color-coding on if you want it to be visible in the Outliner or Binder. In the Menu go to View > Use Label Color In to customize it to your liking. I like the Icons option (pictured above).

Status

Status can be used however you like. Add statuses until they match your writing process. Scrivener comes with decent defaults, but don't be afraid to customize it. Need four drafts before the final? Want to have a "Waiting on Editorial Feedback" or "Beta read" status? Great! Add them.

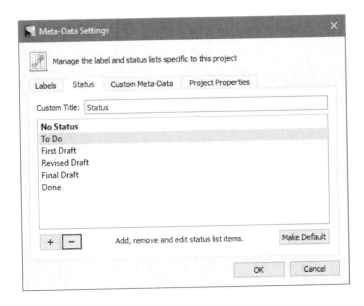

Both Labels and Statuses are also editable on each scene in the General section of the Inspector (visible in Notes, References, and Keywords panes). Just open the dropdown you want to change and click **Edit...** at the bottom, it will take you to the Meta-Data Settings pane to edit them.

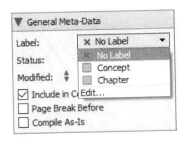

Custom Meta-Data

Custom Meta-Data is the last pane in Meta-Data Settings, and a very powerful one for further customization. You might want to add setting, motivation, or anything else to your outline to stay organized. Make the custom metadata you add visible in the Outliner by clicking the arrow to the right of the column headers of the Outliner and selecting your Custom Meta-Data field to be visible as a column.

It's worth mentioning that I don't use these too much. If you can't find a use for Custom Meta-Data, either, it can be safely ignored.

Custom Icons

The Binder also supports custom icons. To change an icon, right click on a document in the Binder and select **Change Icon** to find this list of available icons:

Reset Icon to Default	
Recent	
Blackboard	
Statistics	
Light Bulb	
Magnifying Glass	
Eye	
Book	▶
Characters	▶
Flag	▶
Locations	▶
Notes	▶
TV	▶
Way-Station	▶
Blackboard	
Clapper Board	
Eye	
Figures and Graphs	
Front Matter	
Information	
Lectern	
Light Bulb	
Magnifying Glass	
Reviewer Comments	
Speech Bubble	
Statistics	
Sync Folder	
Tables	
Test Tube	
Thought Bubble	
To Do	
Warning	
Manage Icons...	

I like to use the icons to differentiate large sections of my project, like Manuscript, Research, Cut Scenes, Sales Copy, and Outline.

There are plenty of icons to keep you happy, but if you want to add your own custom icons you can do so by going to **Documents > Change Icon > Manage Icons...** from the Menu. You'll need to use a supported icon image format, so don't do try this unless you're familiar with digital imaging formats and software like Photoshop or Illustrator.

I find that the icons that come with Scrivener provide plenty of options to suit my daily writing needs.

Folders and Subfolders

Finally, keep in mind that the Binder is extremely flexible, and you can add as much (or as little) as you want to it. In this document I currently have the following containers: Manuscript, Proposal, Marketing, Competition, Outline/Chapter Synopsis, Notes, Ideas, and Research. And that's not even counting all the files.

Don't let yourself get overwhelmed. Collapse folders for easy viewing, create organizational systems to make your life easier (and your mind clearer), and drag and drop to move files and folders around.

How to Revise Your Story

Once your first draft is complete, your next order of business is to revise it.

Most authors go through several drafts. I typically write at least four drafts of a story, and I read it dozens of times. Everyone is different, but for the beginners out there, a warning: don't make the mistake of thinking your first draft is anywhere near good enough for publication. Writers are terrible judges of their own work, myself included.

Fortunately, Scrivener's Snapshot function and other revision features take a lot of the fear out of revising by giving you a way to capture your draft. You can then add comments, make revisions, and easily revert back if the changes you made don't work like you hoped.

Rest Your Manuscript

First of all, you finished a draft: Congratulations! It's time to celebrate.

You've still got a lot of work to do, but it's important to celebrate the small victories. Go out with your friends. Open a nice bottle of wine. Treat yourself to a massage to work out the cramped neck muscles you acquired from bending over your laptop and typing furiously as you flew toward the end of your story.

Before you dig into your revisions, I suggest taking at least a week to rest your manuscript. Possibly longer, but no more than a couple months. How long you can afford to rest it is entirely dependent on your own process and level of comfort, but don't sit idle in the meantime. Write a couple short stories or start another book to keep your craft muscles fit and your mind engaged.

Taking space and time off is the only way to see your manuscript with fresh eyes without enlisting the help of others. While you're away, your subconscious mind will work on it without the necessity for active thought. New ideas will occur to you in the oddest places—in the shower, at the gym, in bed before you fall asleep. Subconscious thinking is one wonderful aspect of the human brain.

When you're ready, sit down and open your story with a positive outlook.

Now, the real work begins.

Take Snapshots

Whether you just finished draft one or you are about to start draft four, kick off each revision with a Snapshot of every scene. Unfortunately, you can't take a Snapshot of an entire Scrivener project in a single click. You'll have to go through scene by scene and take individual Snapshots. It will only take a few minutes and will be well worth the effort.

To take Snapshots, start at your first scene, and open the Snapshots pane of your Inspector. (The button to open it looks like a little camera.) Click the plus (+) at the top (or in the Menu select **Documents > Snapshots > Take Snapshot**). Then name your Snapshot after your draft version. If this is the first Snapshot, call it something like "Draft 1." You'll thank yourself for naming them in later drafts, when you have multiple Snapshots of each scene.

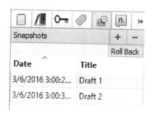

With every scene captured, you now have an undo button for your story; you can safely revise without fear of losing work or screwing something up.

If you ever need to revert back to your Snapshot, simply navigate to the Snapshots pane, select the draft you want to revert back to, and click the **Roll Back** button. You can't undo a Roll Back, so make sure you take another Snapshot before going through with it, just in case you change your mind. Scrivener will remind you to take a Snapshot if you try to Roll Back.

Resolve Your Comments and Annotations

Is the fear of revising going away yet?

Next, you'll want to resolve all of those Document Notes, Comments, and Inline Annotations you added during the messy drafting phase.

Remember how you can click the Comments to jump to their location in the text? That's a handy feature here. Start with the easy ones you know how to resolve, thanks to the time you took to rest your manuscript and all the work your subconscious has done in the meantime. Click on the Comment to jump to it, and then fix whatever was bothering you during your draft.

Don't worry if it's not a perfect fix. Just resolve the inconsistency, error, or missing research. Then delete the comment and move on. If you find yourself agonizing over word choice or grammar, snap yourself out of it. There will be plenty of time for copyediting and proofreading later. Focus on filling in the gaps and getting your story onto the page.

Also resolve all of your Document Notes (if you took any) and Inline Annotations.

We'll go over advanced search techniques in the Scrivener Tips for Pros chapter, but since you're resolving Inline Annotations now, it's worth mentioning that you can find them easily using the search function. In the Menu, go to **Edit > Find > Find by Formatting...** and select "Inline Annotations" from the dropdown. Neat, right?

Red Pen Read-Through

Now that all of the Comments and Annotations are resolved and any gaps you left during your first draft are filled, you're ready for the first full read-through.

I like to print out my story and do a full read-through on paper. Reading on paper is better for your eyes than reading on a screen, and seeing the story in a different medium reveals flaws I missed on the computer.

To print, you can simply open the Manuscript folder and go to **File > Print Current Document**, or you can Compile the Manuscript to Word or PDF and print it out that way (Compile instructions are located in the next chapter).

In any case, sit down with your story and a red pen and start reading. Mark all the issues you see, including word choice, grammar, character motivation, and stilted dialogue. Be ruthless. This is your chance to be critical of your own work.

And take your time. This is not a process that can be rushed.

Once your read-through is complete, import all the changes you made back into Scrivener. Make changes directly to the text, and add bigger issues that still need work as Comments.

(If you prefer not to print out the story, do your full read-through in Scrivener and instead of a red pen, simply add Comments. The end result will be the same; it's simply a matter of preference.)

At the end of this process, you will have made a lot of changes, and you'll have dozens of new comments to resolve. Don't forget to take a new Snapshot!

Drag and Drop to Restructure

You might already have started to make structural changes during your red pen read-through.

That's good. You will want to make those big structural changes first. There's nothing worse than fiddling for hours with sentences and paragraphs only to realize that the scene you were working on actually has no place in the story and needs to be cut.

A successful revision is a matter of getting the structure right *first*. Perhaps one of your POV characters doesn't have a complete arc and they need several new scenes. Maybe you wrote chapters in an order that doesn't support continually rising action or increased stakes, or you wrote past the climax of a scene, or a scene is in the wrong chapter, or ... you get the point.

Scrivener makes the structural edit easier than ever, and this is one of the great advantages of breaking your story down into scenes in the Binder early in the planning phase. Instead of cutting and pasting big chunks of text like you might have done in a linear word processor, you can *drag and drop scenes within the Binder to rearrange them*.

The first task I'll undertake after my red pen read-through is to restructure the story, if necessary. I make new text documents for missing scenes, rearrange the ones that are there so they're in the proper order, and validate my structure with what I know about story craft.

Revise Your Story Free of Fear

Now that you've fixed the structure of your story, you're ready to revise. Everyone has their own method for revising a story, so I'm not going to tell you what to do first other than to reiterate that you should make the large changes up front. Fix the big problems first, and save the small fiddly issues for later.

Delete comments and annotations as you resolve them. Snapshot again after you finish revising a scene. Take as many Snapshots as you need. Knowing your work is saved and version-controlled will allow you to revise free of fear.

You can revert back to a previous Snapshot if whatever change you made during the revision process didn't have the effect you intended.

Version Entire Projects

For drafts where you are doing a lot of rewriting (as opposed to the less intensive *revising*), or where you suspect the end result might be a totally different story and not even Snapshots put your mind at ease, go ahead and duplicate the Scrivener project.

I name my projects with version numbers (1.0, 1.1, 2.0, 2.1, 2.2, etc.) when I duplicate a file. For example, my first novel started out as a short story (1.0), which I revised heavily (1.1). When I started expanding it into a novel, I duplicated the file (2.0) so that I could make huge changes and expansions without losing the work I had already done. Versioning my story went a long way to setting my mind at ease.

I finished the book at version 2.3.

How to Compile Your Story

Once your story is revised and you're happy with the way the current draft turned out, it's time to share it with the world.

Whether you plan to submit it to an agent, send it to an editor, run it by your beta readers, or publish the book, you'll be using Compile to generate the files you need.

More than just printing or saving, Compile is the process by which you lay out your story and export it in the desired format. Using this robust feature you can generate files such as ebooks (.epub, .mobi), Word documents (.doc or .docx), Rich Text files (.rtf), PDFs (for printing and/or print book interior), and other file types.

Compile is One of Scrivener's Most Powerful Features

Why is Compile so powerful?

Say you're one of those writers who likes to customize your Editor. The fonts and margins have to be *just right*. Or maybe you like a black background and green text—it makes you feel like you're in *The Matrix*.

If you wrote a short story and planned on submitting it to a magazine, this format would be unacceptable by their standards. Most magazines only accept stories for submission in Standard Manuscript Format—Courier font, 12 point, double spaced, with page number and last name in the top right corner. (If you aren't familiar with Standard Manuscript Format, you can find examples online.[19])

SCRIVENER SUPERPOWERS

With Scrivener, you can customize your Editor to your heart's content *because Compile removes formatting from the equation.* You simply go to **File > Compile...**, select "Standard Manuscript Format," fill out any missing information, and *voila!* You have a manuscript in Standard Format, and you can still enjoy your crazy *Matrix*-style Editor.

Compiling for Submission and Publication

The second reason Compile is powerful is that it will save you a lot of effort in the digital publishing world.

If you're submitting short stories to magazines, for instance, you probably know that all magazines have different rules about what file types they accept for submission. If they take electronic submissions, sometimes they'll ask for a .docx, sometimes only a .doc. Sometimes they'll take a PDF; other times they'll require an RTF file. Sheesh! With so many options, how are you supposed to make everyone happy?

Compile will help. It allows you to simply and painlessly save your story in any format you could possibly need with relatively little effort.

If you're self-publishing, this is a game changer. No longer do you need to hire someone to format your ebooks and print-on-demand files for the various retailers. You can do it all with Scrivener, and upload the files you generate directly to distributors like Kindle Direct Publishing at Amazon, Kobo, Nook, iBooks, etc.

Compiling for an Editor or Proofreader

Whatever kind of work you're doing, you're likely working with an editor.

Independent authors submit directly to an editor. If you get picked up by a traditional publisher, you'll have to submit your manuscript to an agent first, and later to an editor at the publishing house.

However you get there, if you are working with an editor, they'll probably want your manuscript in a format that allows them to track changes.

In my experience, this means Microsoft Word. It's not ideal, but it's still the preferred tool for tracking changes.

Not that you can't have an editor leave comments and suggest changes directly in Scrivener using a combination of Comments and Snapshots. You certainly can do that, if your editor is willing. This book has already taught you how—just use the same process we discussed in the chapter on revision, but do it with two people.

However, Microsoft Word's change tracking features are simply more robust when it comes to editing. They give you a way to accept/reject changes, to see the edits, and to allow multiple people to track changes in the same document.

After your editor makes their changes and leaves comments in your Word document, you'll want to bring the comments and changes back into Scrivener for your next revision. I go through the manuscript one page at a time and carry the changes over to Scrivener manually. Two reasons: one, I want to learn from my editor's work; two, I like to stay organized.

You may also copy and paste the text back into Scrivener (after you take a Snapshot, of course). Any comments remaining in the Word document will be carried into Scrivener. The suggested changes, however, will not make it over, so use this approach with caution.

Compiling for Beta Readers

You might also want to export your story for your beta readers. It's important to give beta readers the best experience possible, which is why I Compile my story in various formats and send it to them in the format they prefer. For instance, say that one likes to use Word, another prints it out, and a third likes to read on their iPad. I might send a .docx to the first person, a PDF to the second, and an .epub or .mobi file to the third.

You want your readers to be happy. Give them what they want. In turn, they'll read your story and give you the feedback you ask for.

Compile is a Rules-Based Generator

By now you should have given some thought to what files you want to use Compile to generate. Now let's take a moment to talk about what Compile is.

The best way to think about Compile is as a rules-based generation system.

What does that mean? Basically, Compile takes your Scrivener project and generates your desired file based on the rules you provide to the Compiler. In that way, it's a lot like a programming compiler. If you've ever programmed before, you'll pick up Compile pretty quickly. If not, you may have to be a little more patient because it requires a mode of thinking you're probably not used to, especially if you learned to format books another way (like in Word).

There are benefits and drawbacks to the rules-based approach. On the one hand, it removes some of the elements of human error. For instance, your chapter titles and section breaks each have their own rules, so they will always be formatted consistently. On the other hand, it also means that you have to set up your book in a consistent way from the beginning.

Compile is *not* good for all books. Some books you'll have a lot of trouble formatting in Scrivener are children's books and books with lots of visuals and text wrapping.

For novels, short stories, and most nonfiction, Compile works like a charm.

Compile, Summary Tab

Now that you know whom you're compiling for and what file type you need, let's go into the Compile process in more detail.

Start by going to **File > Compile...** to bring up the Compile options workflow. This is the first screen you'll see, the "Summary" of the Compile process.

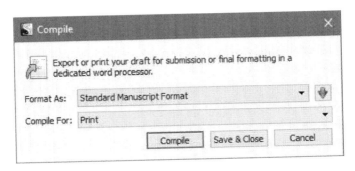

As you can see in the screenshot, I've selected the preset "Standard Manuscript Format" as my desired format. By default, this makes the "Compile For" dropdown below select "Print." If I clicked Compile now, it would open the print screen on my computer, where I could print the book or save it to my computer.

You may change the file type output using the "Compile For" dropdown to generate another type of file, such as a Word Doc, RTF, PDF, or ebook.

If I change the "Format As" preset to generate an ebook, the "Compile For" dropdown will change to "ePub eBook (.epub)." In this screenshot, I have a Kindle format selected as the output:

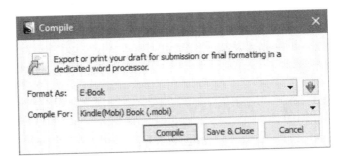

Clicking Compile here would generate a .mobi file that I could upload to Amazon.

All Options Tab

Once you've mastered the presets and are ready to customize your formatting and generated files to your liking, click the blue arrow on the right of the "Format As" dropdown to expand the rest of the options. You should now see this screen:

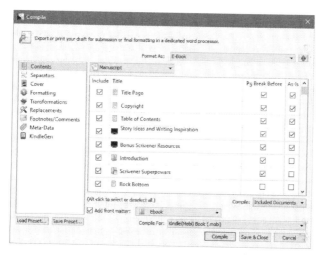

You can still use formatting presets here (the dropdown in the top right), but now you have a lot more options. In the screenshot above, I've chosen to stick to the preset "E-book" and generate a "Kindle eBook (.mobi)" file. (Note: for Kindle books, you'll need to install KindleGen.)

Each file type you choose to generate exposes a different set of Compilation Options (listed in the column on the left). Kindle eBook files have more Compilation Options than most. For comparison, check out the differences in the list when you choose to generate a Plain Text file:

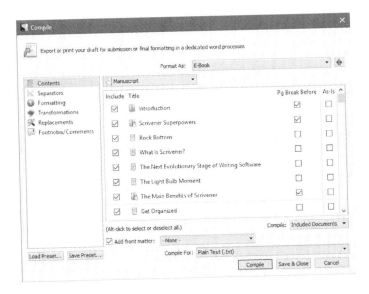

Once you start making significant changes, don't be surprised if the "Format As" dropdown changes to "Custom." It confused me the first time it happened (because I was fiddling with the settings so much), but it's totally normal. Once you begin to actually customize the Compiler for the options you need, you're no longer using a built-in preset, but your own "Custom" settings.

Other Compile Presets

So far on the Summary pane of Compile we've used two presets: Standard Manuscript Format and E-Book.

Scrivener provides several other Compile presets. To see them all, click the "Load Preset..." button in the bottom left of the Compile screen to bring up this window:

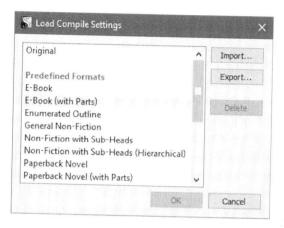

The presets that come with Scrivener are pretty comprehensive and provide the formats that most people need. You can, however, also import and export presets from here. If you find yourself using the same custom Compile options for all of your books, you might want to consider creating a preset to save yourself repeated effort.

For beginners, I recommend using the presets that come with Scrivener. They do a lot of the hard work for you and are a good place to start learning how Compile works. Save your book in the format of your choice, open it to see how it looks, and make adjustments from there.

Contents Pane

Close the presets window to return to the Compile screen.

Let's take look at the rest of the Compilation Options now, starting with the Contents pane.

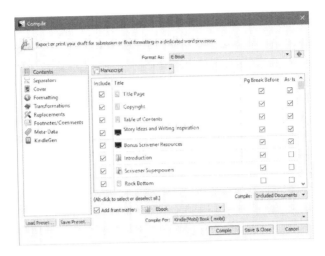

There are two dropdowns on the Contents pane that weren't shown previously.

- **Compile dropdown.** This is where you choose the folders/documents to include in the generated file. In the above screenshot, I've got the Manuscript folder selected. That's usually what you'll want there.

- **Front Matter dropdown.** This is where you choose which folder or file you're using for your front matter. For Standard Manuscript Format, this means simply a title page. I have an entire folder for an Ebook selected above. What you select here depends what you want to be displayed at the front of your book.

The list in the middle is where the interface gets a little more confusing. From the left, let's go through the columns:

- **Include checkbox.** This is asking whether or not you want to include this document in the generated file. You can include/exclude files with finer control here. This is a very useful feature, especially when you're generating ebooks with slightly different Front Matter for different retailers.

- **Title.** The title of the document in question. Nothing to change here.

- **Page Break Before.** This checkbox is asking whether you want the generated file to include a page break before the beginning of the item in question. Notice how I've chosen to include a page break before the beginning of each chapter. That's standard practice in book formatting. You want some white space to give the reader a breather between chapters, and a chance to reflect on what they've just read.

- **As-Is.** Compile will ignore the formatting settings of your Editor unless you check the "As-Is" box. If you check this box, the *exact* formatting you put in your Editor will be carried over to the Compiled file. I use this option for title pages, copyright pages, table of contents pages, or any other pages where the formatting needs to be precise and blank space must be preserved. Copyright pages, for instance, often have blank space at the top of them. This option is also very useful when generating print books, whose formatting is more exact than ebooks.

Separators Pane

The next Compilation Options pane is called Separators.

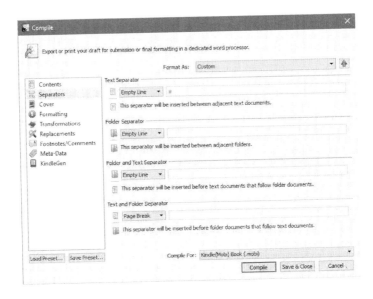

In this section you can specify what you want to insert between sections. You can specify the separator for text documents, folders, folders and text, and text and folders.

There's a description below each one so that you don't get confused. For instance, a text separator "will be inserted between adjacent text documents."

In novels, this is the marker denoting scene breaks. Some authors like to use an empty line (and I've got "Empty line" selected above). Others prefer three asterisks, or three dots, or a pound sign. Type the separator you want to use into the field.

Cover Pane

The next Compilation Options pane for ebooks is Cover. You simply choose your cover image here.

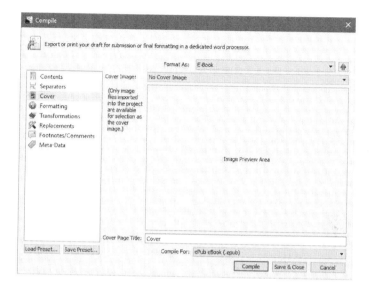

You won't have the Cover pane if you're generating a file without a cover, like a Word Doc or a Plain Text file.

Formatting Pane

The next pane is Formatting. This one is where a lot of your customization will occur, and it's where an understanding of the rules-based generation system makes a big difference.

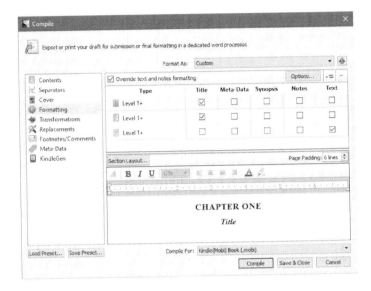

Section Type List

In the list taking up the top half of the Formatting pane, you'll see three rows with icons: a folder, a group of documents, and a single document. They all say "Level 1+" next to them, which denotes their document's level of nesting within the binder.

This hierarchy is important. The corresponding folders/files to which the rules of this item apply depend on their level of nesting. Documents in the root of the Binder correspond to Level 1+. Documents nested beneath those will be labeled Level 2+, etc.

What this means is that any rules you apply to that list item will be applied, in the generation of the file, to all of the items of the same type and level.

You can add and remove levels of hierarchy for complex manuscripts using the +/- buttons at the top right of the pane.

Section Type List Options

The checkboxes to the right of each list item (Title, Meta-Data, Synopsis, Notes, and Text) allow you to choose what gets added for each file/folder item during Compile. In the screenshot above, each chapter and group of files will show only the title, while each single file will show only the text of that file.

For this book, I'm relying on the names of the files to show the subheadings within my chapters. When I Compile, I make sure that the Title and Text checkboxes are ticked for all single documents and groups of documents. That way Compile will automatically generate my chapter titles and sub-headers consistently and with a minimal amount of effort.

Section Formatting

The bottom half of the Formatting pane allows you to customize the text and font styles for each item in the top half of the list. For instance, here's what it looks like when you choose to show only the text of a document with no title.

The Formatting pane has most of your normal text formatting options, such as alignment, bold/italic/underline, color and highlight, line spacing, font, and size.

The Options Button

There are more concealed options worth pointing out. The first set is hidden in an Options button at the top right of the Formatting pane. The other is behind a Section Layout button in the middle left area. You can see them both indicated in the screenshot below.

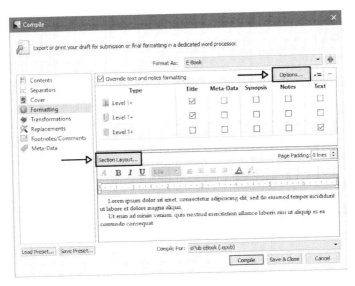

What's behind button number one in the formatting pane, Options?

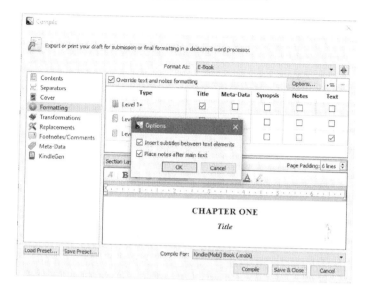

These checkboxes allow you to "Insert subtitles between text elements" and "Place notes after main text."

Section Layout Buttons

The other set of options is hidden behind the Section Layout button. Where the previous Options button is for the entire book, the Section Layout options are unique to each Section Type list item.

It looks like this:

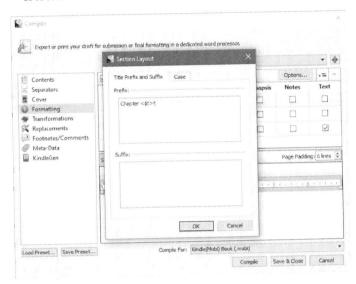

In these options you can:

- **Set Prefixes and Suffixes.** Prefixes are frequently used for auto-numbering chapters, like you see above. The word "Chapter" is typed in, and then the placeholder tag < $t > is used to generate the number of a chapter spelled out, i.e. one, two, three, etc. Note that the prefix and suffix will be displayed even if the title is disabled for this section, which can prove useful in some cases but inconvenient if you don't know about that rule. If you need help with placeholder tags, reference the Scrivener Manual under **Help > Scrivener Manual** and navigate to page 332 (or search for "placeholder tags").

- **Change Case.** In the second tab of the Section Layout Options, you can, for instance, capitalize your titles.

The Formatting pane is very complex. If you need additional assistance, I highly recommend reading the dense but informative Scrivener Help Manual about this section.

Transformations Pane

Next is the Transformations pane, where you'll find several useful options for file-wide overrides.

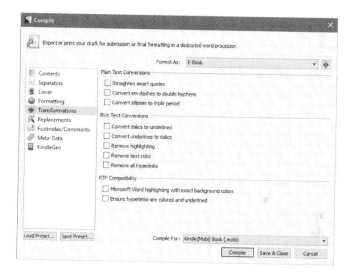

Page Settings Pane

The Page Settings pane is specifically for PDFs.

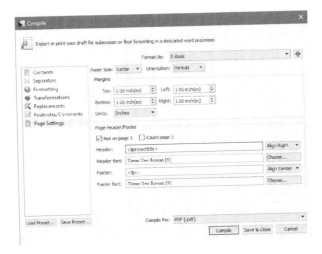

Scrivener can generate PDF files for print book interiors, which you can upload to print-on-demand services like CreateSpace and Lightning Source to create a print version of your book.

On this pane, you specify your margins (dependent on print size), your page header and footer, header/footer font choices, and more.

While you'll need to go to a more robust design program like InDesign for complex print layouts, these Page Settings will allow you to format simple novels, short stories, and nonfiction manuscripts. I used it for my first novel with great success, and it kept me from having to spend money on a formatter to get what I wanted.

Meta-Data Settings

Replacements and Footnotes are pretty straightforward and not used that often, so let's skip down to the Meta-Data pane next, which is used only for ebooks but very important. This is where you enter the title, author, and other information for your book.

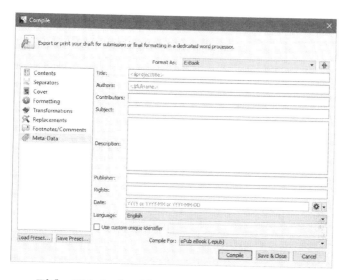

- **Title.** This is the title of your book that is shown on the ereader. It is automatically filled with the metadata you provided in the Meta-Data Settings we talked about in How to Use Meta-Data and Stay Organized. You can type a new title to override these settings.

- **Authors.** This is where you type your author name(s). This field is also automatically filled out based on your Meta-Data Settings, but you can type something else to override it.

You can fill out the rest of the fields if you feel they are necessary. It's a good practice to fill them all out, but they are not required for publication.

KindleGen

Lastly, to generate .mobi files for Kindle Direct Publishing at Amazon, you need to install the KindleGen script.

Once you select a Kindle eBook from the Compile For dropdown, a KindleGen pane will appear that looks like the screenshot above. Navigate to that pane, click the link to Amazon, and follow the instructions. You'll have to install the KindleGen script on your computer and show Scrivener where it is before you can generate a .mobi file.

Book Formatting Services

If Compile intimidates you, stick to the summary screen and the presets and you'll get a working file with a minimal amount of effort. Your ebook might not be perfect, but you can rest assured that it will get the job done.

If formatting simply isn't something you want to do, or you have a more complex book with nuanced formatting needs, locate a professional book formatter. Ask your writer friends for recommendations or contact authors who have well-formatted books and ask them for a referral. It's typically a very affordable service.

Test and Check

To have a good experience with Compile, you'll need to be okay with testing and checking your work. This requires patience and a willingness to do online research when you run into trouble.

In order to check the formatting of an ebook on your computer, make sure you have an app that can read ebooks.

To preview Kindle books, download the Kindle Previewer[20] created by Amazon for independent publishers to check their Kindle files.

I'm also a fan of the Kindle reading apps for testing (and for reading after several drafts have been completed). Kindle apps[21] are available to download on all your computers and devices.

Lastly, the easiest way to get your Kindle files onto your devices for testing or reading is by using the Send To Kindle Email.[23]

Good luck!

Scrivener Tips for Pros

Next, I will show you several methods for importing content, a detailing of Scrivener's search functionality, and how to configure automated backups.

These advanced tips aren't required for the start-to-finish writing process we've covered in the previous chapters, but if you spend a lot of time in Scrivener, they will help you work better and more efficiently.

Importing Content

If you've got a lot of material stored in formats other than Scrivener and wish to move the content over to Scrivener, you have a few options.

These methods are useful whether you're importing your own work or if you're using Scrivener to format a book written by someone else in another word processor.

Copy and Paste

Option number one: Go through your original document, whether that's a Microsoft Word file or something else, and copy and paste the text one section at a time into corresponding files in a new Scrivener project.

Or, you can dump the whole manuscript into a single text document, and split it up in Scrivener after you close the other program.

Copying and pasting can be tedious and time consuming, but

I find that it's the most reliable method for transferring content into Scrivener.

Nothing is lost or missing or broken because I oversee the transfer myself.

Import

Your second option, a more automated method, is to use the Import function found in the Menu under **File > Import > Files...**

This is a suitable alternative if you can't stomach a copy and paste session, but it's far from perfect. Import's job is simply to get the content into Scrivener, relying on the user to sort out the organization later.

In my opinion, you're better off copying and pasting the content into Scrivener manually.

Import and Split

You third and final option is somewhere between a manual and an automated process. It's called Import and Split, and you can find it in the Menu under **File > Import > Import and Split...**

This function asks you to determine what the "Sections are separated by:" in the file selection menu, and then breaks those sections out into separate files during the import.

For instance, let's say you have a novel manuscript in Microsoft Word, and your novel is broken down into 20 chapters.

What you do is go through *the original document* and place a unique marker at the end of each chapter that tells the Import and Split function where to create a new file in the Scrivener project during import.

Say you use three pound signs as the unique marker. First, make sure ### is not present anywhere else in the manuscript except where you want the file breaks to occur. Then, after making sure ### is at the end of each chapter:

1. Click on the folder you want to import the content to
2. Select **Import and Split...** from the Menu
3. Type your marker, ###, in the "Sections are separated by:" input
4. Choose your file from the file selection menu
5. Press enter.

Scrivener will then automatically break your 20 chapters out into separate files based on where you inserted the unique split marker.

If it doesn't break how you'd expect, simply delete the files from your Scrivener project and try again.

More Work Now, Less Headache Later

I hope you don't find the task of importing content into Scrivener a chore. It causes a little extra work now, but less headache in the long run, like straightening that paper-strewn desk in your office before you start writing, or cleaning out the junk drawer in your kitchen that always seems to fill up so quickly.

In other words, it's worth the effort.

Advanced Search

Advanced Search is one of my favorite features in Scrivener. It has saved me many headaches in the revision stage by helping me locate troublesome words and phrases (e.g. "the fact that", "that said", "was" and other weak words and phrases), find particular pieces of research material, and change names across entire projects.

Find

You can access all of the search functions in the Menu under Edit > Find. There, you'll find the following options:

- Find...
- Find Next
- Find Previous
- Use Selection for Find
- Jump to Selection
- Project Replace...
- Project Search...
- Find by Formatting...
- Find Next by Formatting
- Find Previous by Formatting

I'm not going to cover the Find functions you are likely familiar with (Find..., Find Next, Find Previous), and which come standard with many software programs, except to say that the normal search and replace function can be located in the **Find...** menu.

Project Search

What's far more interesting and useful are Scrivener's project-wide search and replace functions.

Because Scrivener is a nonlinear word processing tool, the normal Find function is limited to searching and replacing *only the current document*.

When you want to do a project-wide search/replace, you'll want to use the Project Search or Project Replace functions instead.

You can access the Project Search two ways: by locating **File > Project Search...** in the Menu, or by typing into the search field in the Toolbar.

When you type into the search field, your Binder (the left-hand column in Scrivener) is replaced with your search results. It looks something like this:

The searched phrase is highlighted in the Editor, and you can use the Binder to jump between search results to quickly find what you're looking for.

To exit out of the search, click the X in the search bar.

Project Replace

Project Replace allows you to do a search and replace across an entire project.

Going to **File > Find > Project Replace...** in the Menu brings up this screen:

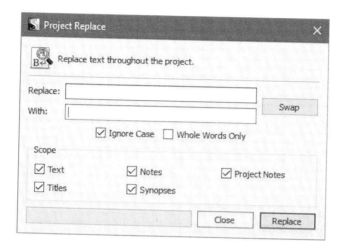

I've used the Project Replace with great success when:

- Changing names of characters across entire manuscripts
- Changing names of settings/locations
- Changing placeholder annotations or phrases to the final chosen phrase.

The extra options are fantastic for narrowing your search and replace by case, and to specific portions of text (e.g. you can uncheck Titles to exclude them from the search and replace).

Other Advanced Search Options

Finally, the last search option worth mentioning is Find by Formatting, which allows you to search everything else: highlighted text, comments and footnotes, inline annotations, links, and more.

Automated Backups

Always, always, *always* back up your work.

In the past two days I've seen Facebook posts from two writers whose computers died. They lost large chunks of manuscripts they were working on.

They were both horrified and distraught. Don't let that happen to you!

To make your life easier and less stressful, Scrivener supports automatic backups. It's like magic!

Simply navigate to the Backup pane of your Options, and configure what you find there:

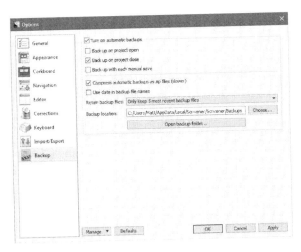

Super easy, right?

Don't forget to point the Backup location to a place where you'll remember how to find it later, if you need it. I'm a big fan of putting my Backup location in a folder in Dropbox for an added measure of security.

Let me explain: The desktop app of a cloud-storage service like Dropbox essentially puts a folder on your computer that is automagically synced to "the cloud." That means that there's a copy of those files on your computer, and another copy in "the cloud," which is a fancy way of saying, "file servers on the other side of the world."

If you don't know what the cloud is, don't worry too much. What's important is that when your files are in the cloud, even if your computer breaks or catches fire or spontaneously combusts, your files are still safe and accessible. If my computer exploded *right now*, I could borrow a friend's computer, log into my Dropbox account on the web, download my most recent backups, and return to work five minutes later (as long as I had a new computer to use that wasn't on fire).

Even with my files backed up this way, I store a redundant copy of all of my work (an entire folder called "Stories" roughly 1GB in size) on an external hard drive. That means the files are on my computer, on Dropbox, *and* on an external drive. Three copies is the minimum required for safety.

You can get a Dropbox account with 2GB of space for free. That's plenty of space to store a few Scrivener backups of your latest manuscript, plus some of your other files, too.

External hard drives can be purchased for less than $100 (sometimes significantly less, especially if you only need a small thumb drive) at any electronics store.

Don't tempt existential terror. Back up your work.

PART 5

Additional Resources

Amplify Your Word Count

In How to Set Targets and Measure Your Progress, I covered how Scrivener can help you set word count targets, why you should keep track of your word count, and a few pieces of advice that will help you write more, faster.

There are a lot of books and resources out there to help you improve in this area. These are a few of my favorites.

2k to 10k by Rachel Aaron, mentioned previously, changed my entire view of word counts. Her methods for how she writes better and faster are culled from hard-won experience. Since they come from the mind of a professional writer, they're also extremely actionable. Additionally, the short little book is only 99 cents on Kindle, so it's a great value.

Another great book is *Take Off Your Pants!* by Libbie Hawker. This one is unique because it explains the benefits and techniques for plotting and planning a book to write faster. It's another successful author's perspective on amplifying your word count.

If you're a little bit more technical and also want an app to do some of the heavy lifting for you, I recommend you check out Chris Fox's *5,000 Words Per Hour* and the accompanying iOS app. It's like a pomodoro timer built specifically for writers that times your sessions and calculates useful figures like words per hour to measure your gains.

Though I haven't tried it myself, I've heard that learning to use voice dictation to write will add another layer of awesome to your word-count-crushing abilities. *Dictate Your Book* by Monica Leonelle goes into detail about how one author uses dictation to reach 4,000 words per hour as a regular order of business.

Finally, National Novel Writing Month, or NaNoWriMo, is a yearly competition that takes place in November and challenges writers to type out the first draft of a novel, a full 50,000 words, in a single month. If you break it down, that's 1,667 words per day. The true advantage of NaNoWriMo is in the community—there are local chapters in most major cities and online write-a-thons that will ignite your motivation. Get together for write-ins with other writers in your area, check out the pep talks from successful authors online, and stay inspired through the month by tapping into all the NaNoWriMo resources.

My No Nonsense Novel Template

Scrivener comes with two standard templates for novels. As usual, I wasn't satisfied with the way they set the templates up, so I added several tools and created my own.

Here's what you'll find in my No Nonsense Novel Template (it can also be used for short stories):

- Character and Setting sketch template sheets
- Front Matter for Standard Manuscript Format, ebook, and print book
- Research folder
- Sales copy folder
- Six Core Competencies[24] folder
- Nine Point Outline folder (tip of the hat to *Story Engineering* by Larry Brooks)
- Characters folder
- Settings folder
- Cut Scenes folder
- Template Sheets folder
- Icons for each of the top-level folders

You can download this template on my website at scrivenersuperpowers.com/no-nonsense-novel-template.

Lester Dent's Pulp Paper Master Fiction Plot Template

In addition to my own novel template, I'd also like to recommend the Scrivener template created by Lou Yuhasz[25] based on Lester Dent's Pulp Paper Master Fiction Plot.

Lester Dent was a pulp writer in the 1930s famous for his Doc Savage stories. Like many writers of that time period, he made a living writing short fiction and selling it to pulp magazines. Because this sort of job required a steady output of quality stories, Lester Dent put together what he called his "Pulp Paper Master Fiction Plot" to guide his plotting and planning efforts, create a framework for quality, and generally make his job a little bit easier.

I've used this plot outline myself, and find it very effective. Incredibly enough, Lester Dent suggests using a four-part structure, a common approach espoused by other modern teachers of story craft like Larry Brooks and a structure that harkens back to ancient times.

Try it out on a new story. You might enjoy the challenge. While some writers feel that having any sort of "prescriptive" guide limits their creativity, I find the exact opposite: having guidelines allows me to be more creative.

If you still aren't sure, ask yourself this question: Is it still art if it doesn't have a frame?

How to Make Your Own Scrivener Templates

When you download a template in Scrivener, it comes in the format of any other Scrivener project.

Two important distinctions: for Windows, the Scrivener project is an entire folder; for Mac, it's a single file.

Once you have the template downloaded, add it to your stored templates from which you create new projects by doing the following:

1. Open the Scrivener file.
2. In the Menu, go to **File > Save As Template...**
3. Add a unique and recognizable Title, Category, Description, and Icon.
4. Click "OK."

Boom, you have a new template!

Now, when you go to **File > New Project...** you will see the new template as an option, organized by the Category you chose in step three above.

Experiment with your own templates, and let me know if you've created an awesome one that's worth sharing.

Further Reading Recommendations

There are a ton of fabulous books out there that you can read to improve your craft, your grammar, and your know-how as a writer.

Here is a long list of my favorites.

Story Craft
- *Writing Fiction: A Guide to Narrative Craft* by Janet Burroway
- *Story Engineering* by Larry Brooks
- *Story Physics* by Larry Brooks
- *The Modern Library Writer's Workshop* by Stephen Koch
- *Plot and Structure* by James Scott Bell
- *Writing in General and the Short Story in Particular* by Rust Hills
- *2k to 10k* by Rachel Aaron
- *On Writing* by Stephen King
- *Let's Write a Short Story* by Joe Bunting
- *Write Good or Die* by many authors (edited by Scott Nicholson)
- *On Writing Well* by William Zinsser
- *Bird by Bird: Some Instructions on Writing and Life* by Anne Lamott
- *Story Grid: What Good Editors Know* by Shawn Coyne

Grammar

- *The Elements of Style* by William Strunk, Jr.
- *Eats, Shoots & Leaves: The Zero Tolerance Approach to Punctuation* by Lynne Truss
- *The Chicago Manual of Style*
- *The Associated Press Stylebook 2015*

Indie Publishing

- *Let's Get Digital: How To Self-Publish, And Why You Should* by David Gaughran
- *Let's Get Visible: How To Get Noticed And Sell More Books* by David Gaughran
- *Write. Publish. Repeat. (The No-Luck-Required Guide to Self-Publishing Success)* by Johnny B. Truant, Sean Platt, and David Wright
- *Business For Authors: How To Be An Author Entrepreneur* by Joanna Penn

You can find links to read or purchase all of these titles on my website at scrivenersuperpowers.com/further-reading-recommendations-for-writers.

About the Author

Born in 1988, my full name is Matthew Gilbert Herron. I write science fiction fantasy under the pen name M. G. Herron. My friends call me Matt.

Books and reading have always been close to my heart. I love epic fantasies and fast-paced action adventure novels. My passion for literature, the dusty vanilla smell of old paperbacks, and turns of phrase that prickle your skin eventually led me into writing, and I now earn my living as freelance writer and storyteller.

I currently live in Austin, TX with my girlfriend, Shelly, and our dog, Elsa.

You can find a full list of my books, sign up for my fan list, and read my blog at mgherron.com.

Twitter: @mgherron
Facebook: facebook.com/mgherronauthor
Email: matt@mgherron.com

Scrivener Resources

This book is just one piece of a larger set of resources and tools I've built to help you transform your writing practice.

To access bonus content, templates, author interviews, and video tutorials, go to the book's website, scrivenersuperpowers.com.

See you there!

Want to Become a Writer?

Learn what it takes to turn your writing ambitions into a lifestyle. Get the free 10-step guide from The Write Practice.

Download the guide instantly at http://thewritepractice.com/writer.

"Gave me more food for thought than any other advice I have been given." —Reader Review

#1 Amazon Bestseller

All the great writers started with short stories. Shouldn't you be writing them, too? Take your dreams of a writing career and turn them into practical steps with *Let's Write a Short Story*, the entertaining and empowering guide to the art and business of writing short stories.

Get the book here: letswriteashortstory.com/purchase.

"Few people understand the art of fiction writing as well as my friend Joe Bunting." —Jeff Goins

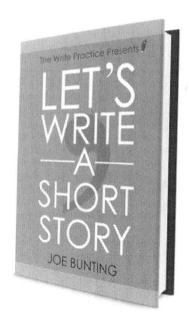

Notes and References

[1] literatureandlatte.com/scrivener.php, December 2015

[2] For an explanation of the concept of the infinite canvas, go to http://scottmccloud.com/4-inventions/canvas/index.html.

[3] To view Joanna Penn's full interview, go to https://www.youtube.com/watch?v=Wq9I3rdqQvM.

[4] To view Garrett Robinson's full interview, go to https://www.youtube.com/watch?v=UaoT-Nq9gvk.

[5] To view Gwen Hernandez's full interview, go to https://www.youtube.com/watch?v=IzJUAjpAs8Y.

[6] To view Joe Bunting's full interview, go to https://www.youtube.com/watch?v=58vXXrrnMPs.

[7] To view Rachel Aaron's full interview, go to https://www.youtube.com/watch?v=hPyvSHqIPxk.

[8] To view Simon Whistler's full interview, go to https://www.youtube.com/watch?v=VATPzM7wQ-g.

[9] To download Scrivener for Mac, go to http://literatureandlatte.com/scrivener.php.

[10] Some of my favorite resources for free stock photos include https://unsplash.com/, https://commons.wikimedia.org/wiki/Main_Page, https://www.pexels.com/,

https://pixabay.com/ and https://www.morguefile.com/.

[11] Writer's Digest and literary agent Rachelle Gardner explain what it means to use setting as a character. Learn more at http://www.writersdigest.com/online-editor/how-to-make-your-setting-a-character and http://www.rachellegardner.com/using-setting-as-a-character-a-tip-for-novelists/.

[12] Shawn Coyne of The Story Grid explores how scenes are the basic unit of storytelling at http://www.storygrid.com/the-scene/.

[13] To learn more about rising action, go to http://literarydevices.net/rising-action/.

[14] Learn more about Aeon Timeline at http://www.scribblecode.com/.

[15] For help integrating Aeon Timeline with Scrivener, go to http://www.scribblecode.com/faq_scrivener.html.

[16] https://duotrope.com/

[17] http://thegrinder.diabolicalplots.com/

[18] I blogged about my word count goals and results for my first novel at http://mgherron.com/word-count-first-novel/.

[19] Find an example of Standard Manuscript Format at http://www.shunn.net/format/story.html.

[20] You can download the Kindle Previewer at http://www.amazon.com/gp/feature.html?docId=1000765261.

[21] You can download the Kindle app for all your computers and devices here: http://www.amazon.com/gp/help/customer/display.html?nodeId=200783640.

[22] Learn how to use your Send to Kindle email address at http://www.amazon.com/gp/help/customer/display.html?nodeId=201974220.

[23] To download Scrivener for Windows, go to http://literatureandlatte.com/scrivener.php?platform=win.

[24] To learn about the Six Core Competencies of writing, go to http://www.writersdigest.com/tip-of-the-day/spotlight-on-story-engineering-the-six-core-competencies.

[25] To download Lou Yuhasz's Scrivener template, go to http://www.byzantineroads.info/scrivenerpulptemplate/. To learn about Lester Dent's Pulp Paper Master Fiction Plot, go to http://www.paper-dragon.com/1939/dent.html.

Made in the USA
San Bernardino, CA
24 October 2017